1,001 Symbols

1,001 Symbols

An Illustrated Guide to Imagery and Its Meaning

JACK TRESIDDER

CHRONICLE BOOKS

SAN FRANCISCO

CONTENTS

First published in the United States in
2004 by Chronicle Books, LLC.

Copyright © Duncan Baird Publishers 2003
Text copyright © Jack Tresidder 2003
Commissioned artwork copyright © Duncan
Baird Publishers 2002

Conceived, created and designed by
Duncan Baird Publishers

Library of Congress Cataloging-in-
Publication Data available

ISBN: 0-8118-4282-7

Manufactured in Thailand

Typeset in AT Shannon

Distributed in Canada by Raincoast Books
9050 Shaughnessy Street
Vancouver, British Columbia V6P 6E5

10 9 8 7 6 5 4 3 2

Chronicle Books LLC
85 Second Street
San Fransisco, California 94105

www.chroniclebooks.com

Introduction	6
1 Blessings and Hardships	18
Protection	20
Mortality and Transience	35
Longevity	40
Fertility	43
Fecundity and Plenty	56
Wealth and Prosperity	64
Fame and Fortune	70
Bad Luck	76
Health	80
2 Human Qualities and Powers	86
Power	88
Authority	96
Sovereignty	102
Strength and Stability	108
Masculinity and Virility	114
Femininity and Maternity	122
Beauty and Grace	130
Knowledge and Learning	134
Vigilance and Guardianship	138

3 Virtues and Vices 142

Goodness and Benevolent Power 144
Evil 152
Innocence 164
Truth and Deceit 166
Charity, Care and Compassion 171
Faith and Hope 174
Justice 180
Fortitude and Courage 182
Temperance and Humility 187
Gluttony, Sloth, Avarice
    and Pride 192
Chastity and Virginity 196
Prudence and Wisdom 205
Fidelity and Loyalty 212
Purity and Incorruptibility 216

4 Emotions and Instincts 222

Love 224
Lust 240
Envy and Jealousy 244
Anger and Cruelty 247
Happiness and Joy 250
Grief, Mourning and Melancholia 254
Instinct, Intuition and the
    Unconscious 260

5 States and Conditions 264

Peace and Freedom 266
War and Victory 272
Defeat, Cowardice and
    Betrayal 280
Duality and Union 282
Harmony and Meditation 290
Death 294

6 Spiritual Life 302

Divinity and Sanctity 304
Salvation and Redemption 316
Images of the Soul 322
Immortality and Eternity 325
Rebirth and Resurrection 330
Enlightenment and
    Transformation 340
Ascension and Axial Interchange 348
Purification, Atonement and
    Propitiation 358
Divination 368

Index 374

Acknowledgments 384

INTRODUCTION

Traditional symbols form a universal language which is becoming more mysterious as we move further away from the thought patterns and worldview of those who produced it. Originally, these symbols – typically, familiar objects standing for something abstract, such as an idea, quality, emotion, value, aspiration, belief, hope or fear – were anything but mysterious. Their intention was to provide an instantly recognizable representation, or mental picture, of a concept. Images have always conveyed ideas more swiftly than words, and they predated written words by thousands of years. The pictograms and ideographs that led ultimately to the invention of the alphabet drew on earlier symbols that were used for primitive magical purposes.

Signs and symbols often overlap each other but have different purposes. Whereas signs simply provide information, symbols give ordinary things a larger dimension, often a spiritual one. To take a basic example, a quality such as courage, regarded as a fundamental virtue in the ancient world, was represented by a creature that seemed to embody it – the lion. Once chosen, the strength of the symbol intensified as artists created forceful images of it and it was woven into the whole fabric of a society's life through myth, legend, ritual and architectural or costume decoration. It might also begin to acquire wider meanings.

In Egypt, for example, the lion became more than just a symbol of a human attribute. It was an emblem of the power and majesty of the sun and, by extension, of the pharaoh, who was the sun god's earthly repre- 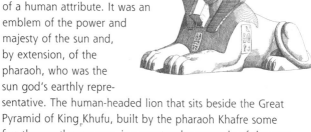 sentative. The human-headed lion that sits beside the Great Pyramid of King Khufu, built by the pharaoh Khafre some five thousand years ago, is a spectacular example of the way in which a symbol could be used to consolidate the dynastic and religious framework that held an entire nation together. Through such powerful symbols and rituals, a priestly class could control society and impose ethical rules on it.

The symbolism of the lion could not only expand outward but also turn inward to the minutiae of daily life. Because the zodiacal lion sign, Leo, represented the sun in its most fiery phase between July and August, the lion was linked with the fertile flooding of the Nile at this time of the year. Given this entirely new connection between the lion and water, it was a short symbolic step to the production of lion-headed fountains for Egyptian palaces and public build- ings. Lion water spouts are just as popular with garden

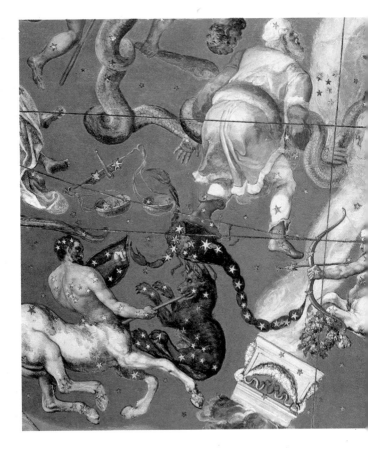

designers today, but their origins and symbolic meaning have been forgotten. Many people must speculate as to why a lion – associated with hot, dry habitats – should preside over a stream of water.

Scores of traditional symbols have a similar history of development, moving from having one meaning to having many. The serpent, an early and fundamental animist symbol of the cosmic life-force animating all things, has at least 20 other emblematic meanings, which vary according to context or culture. Some are positive, others negative. Even the dragon, with which the snake shares some of its symbolism, is ambivalent. It embodies evil in Western tradition, but in Asia is an emblem of fertilizing spring rain – and this is the significance of the paper dragons that are carried or used as masks in Chinese festive processions.

Thus, symbols do not have fixed meanings. To take two famous modern examples: the swastika was once a sign of beneficial cosmic power, and pointing two fingers upward in a "V" sign was insulting. In Hitler's hands, the swastika became a symbol of brutal force; in Churchill's, the "V" symbolized victory against that force because he turned his hand so that his palm was opened towards his audience.

In forming their own language of symbols, different societies often selected the same images from the natural world – particular animals, birds, fish, insects, plants, features of the earth or cosmos – and, to a remarkable degree, the meanings attached to them are similar also. A phenomenon such as lightning suggested in all cultures divine power or wrath, virility and fertility, so that peoples with no knowledge of each other might recognize jagged linear motifs as symbols of these ideas. But the interpretation of other symbols depended on the social, emotional or spiritual needs of specific cultures. The jackal, an embodiment of evil in India, became in Egypt the attribute of a respected underworld deity, Anubis, charged with care of the dead and responsible for ushering souls to judgement.

The thinking behind such a transformation sometimes remains mysterious. In elevating the status of the jackal, were the Egyptians attempting through sympathetic magic to stop jackals raiding graves? Or were they offering a consoling image to families whose graves were desecrated in this way? Symbolism is full of such puzzles, and symbolists often disagree about the origin of a particular emblem. The fish is a famous early symbol of Jesus Christ, and Christian scholars suggest that this was because the letters of the Greek word *ichthus* (fish) formed an acronym for "Jesus Christ, Son of God, Saviour". But was this an ingenious way to validate Christianity's use of a much more ancient pagan symbol for divinity? The Sumerian creator-god Enki was depicted as a man in the guise of a fish.

Differences of interpretation do not make the symbols less valid but they do mean that some knowledge of their cultural origins is needed to appreciate their allusive richness. Many symbols are based on ancient myths and legends, which were transmitted orally before being written down and which are themselves full of symbolic and allegorical significance. For example, myths of powerful contending gods controlling wind and weather at the four main directions of space – north, south, east and west – led to the number four acquiring extraordinary symbolic power throughout much of pre-Columbian America in religious rites directed towards maintaining an advantageous balance between these supernatural forces.

The same number stood much more widely for totality, stability and universal power. The four seasons themselves seemed to support the idea of a cosmic order based on the number four. In many traditions, the repeating cycle of spring, summer, autumn and winter symbolized a pattern of birth, growth, decline, death and regeneration which made sense of the human life-cycle and offered the expectation of rebirth in a spiritual sense if not a physical one. The supreme gods of Egypt and Hindu India were shown with four faces, and Hindu society was organized into four castes, again with the symbolism of order and stability. In the West, an entire symbol system was erected upon the notion of four elements – earth, air, fire and water – being the basis of order and harmony, not only in the cosmos but in the human body. In medieval medicine, physicians assigned physical and temperamental characteristics to each element and sought to harmonize them.

The advance of science has dismantled such obscurantist beliefs. And it is undeniable

that, for all its imaginative and cohesive value in the rise of civilization,
symbolism could have appallingly
harmful consequences when it was
misused. At the height of the Aztec
Empire, the symbolic link between
the sun as the heart of the universe
and the human heart as the body's
"sun" led to 20,000 victims a year
having their hearts ripped from their bodies. These sacrifices were justified as necessary to sustain the sun's energy in its
mythical daily battle with the forces of
darkness. Blood, universally equated with the life-force,
is one of the deepest and darkest of all symbols, as its role
in sacrificial rites shows. It is one of many symbols overlaid
with accretions of primitive animist beliefs, myth, religion,
sympathetic magic and pure superstition.

Science has been influential in eliminating superstition
and belief in magic. It attempts to contain philosophical
thought within a strict framework of space and time, a
universe of physical laws which is indifferent to human life
and morality. Because nothing is provable outside this
framework, the possibility of a spirit that is not contingent

on space and time has begun to seem conceptually outdated or irrelevant. The scientific mind-set is thus very different from the more imaginative and intuitive mind-set of those who developed the language of symbolism over thousands of years.

For the societies from which traditional symbolism emerged, the realm of space and time was penetrated by a higher consciousness, however it might be delineated. The structures of mythology and symbolism which grew out of this belief seemed to offer an explanation of the cosmos and of human life which allowed for the larger context which, until now, humans have felt must exist. The idea that we are born, exist briefly and die answering to no higher power or purpose would have seemed not only unbearable but disastrous. Symbolic community rituals were thought to be essential to keep society in harmony with the rhythms of nature. Everything was interlinked. The individual was not alone.

In other words, life was not the meagre thing it seemed to be, but had a spiritual dimension. Symbolism arose not from intellect but from imagination and a deep sense of identification with the whole cosmos. It had little to do with empirical facts. Its impact was usually visual, sensory and emotional. Symbols based on apt analogies or metaphors and on psychic truths could be reassuring as well as persuasive. People associated with a powerful symbol felt enlarged by it.

To some degree, the same can be said of modern symbols – as is evident in the emblems used by sporting teams. Insignia and badges give a sense of group identification and pride. In television advertising, the human talent for image-making has never been deployed more skilfully to convey concepts by means of images. Symbols of product benefits flashing up on screens and disappearing at almost subliminal speed are nevertheless recognized and understood by mass audiences. But they have shorter and shorter currency as their novelty-value disappears. What underlies them is commerce not belief.

More traditional symbols emerged from a far more stable conceptual universe. Exploring it gives us insights into the development and meaning of the symbols and attributes used in figurative art for hundreds of years. At the same time, it reminds us how strongly people once believed that there was a mystical dimension to life and that the ordinary world could be transcended.

About this book

1001 Symbols is organized more like a thesaurus than a
conventional dictionary. Most reference guides to symbolism
are arranged as alphabetical lists of symbols whose main and
subsidiary meanings are defined and discussed individually.
This book takes a simpler, perhaps more cohesive approach.
It starts from the idea, quality or state symbolized and then
discusses under this topic all the main symbols traditionally
used to represent it. Important symbols with multiple meanings therefore appear under several different topic headings.

Closely related topics are sometimes grouped together.
The aim here is to provide an overview of the various
symbols used by different cultures to stand for concepts
such as Wisdom, Goodness, Evil, Truth, Justice, Chastity,
Grief, Freedom and Salvation.

A few concepts have an unusually large number of
symbols, suggesting their exceptional importance to earlier
societies. Fertility, Fecundity, Protection, Power, Love,
Divinity, Immortality and Rebirth are all notable examples
of categories that have always been a focus for symbolism
in many cultures throughout the world.

Apart from identifying these major preoccupations of
early civilizations, the book shows that traditional symbolism
as a whole was developed to represent a relatively small

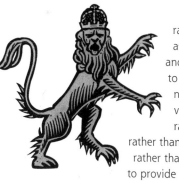

range of ideas which were seen as the keystones of civilization, and that symbols generally tended to emphasize positive rather than negative aspects of existence: virtues rather than vices, hope rather than despair, strength rather than weakness, peace and unity rather than war and discord. They evolved to provide ideals that would inspire respect for authority, social order, cooperation, ethical behaviour, spiritual discipline, resolution in the face of danger and reassurance in death as well as life.

Note on cross-references: Throughout this book, the reader will find boxes with cross-references to other (alternative or divergent) meanings of designated symbols. In each case, the symbol that is the starting point is referred to in the box by its entry number on that page. One or more different meanings of the particular symbol are then indicated by citing the thematic sections and the page numbers on which they occur. Thus, for example, in the section on "Health", the reader is alerted to an alternative meaning for the symbol of the toad given elsewhere in the book: "**196** Evil, p.159".

Blessings and Hardships

Protection 20

Mortality and Transience 35

Longevity 40

Fertility 43

Fecundity and Plenty 56

Wealth and Prosperity 64

Fame and Fortune 70

Bad Luck 76

Health 80

PROTECTION

1 PENTACLE

Survival was so problematic in the ancient world that protective symbols emerged in most cultures to provide people with psychic reassurance. Some of these symbols, like the sign known as the pentacle, began as no more than linear motifs, the origins of which were forgotten but which acquired significance as traditions gathered about them.

The pentacle was eventually, in medieval Europe, thought to have talismanic power to ward off everything from sickness to Satan. The five-pointed star was drawn with one horizontal line and four diagonal oness. It was based on older star signs, probably representing the movements of the planet Venus and evoking her protection. Medieval magicians wore pentacle-shaped caps, and pentacle signs were carved on rock or wood and inscribed on amulets against the evil eye. In India, similar patterns with cosmic significance, but in the form of a six-pointed **hexagram (2)**, are described in powder on village thresholds to ward off hostile spirits of the dead. The pattern is called the Star of Lakshmi, Goddess of Blessings.

3 RINGS

The strength of the circle as an enclosing shape accounts for the protective significance of rings, which are still sometimes credited with semi-magical powers. In legend, the supposed force-field created by a ring was often more powerful if it contained a **precious stone (4)**, as gemstones were once thought to be of supernatural origin. Stones believed to have special protective value include the **diamond (5)**, because its divine radiance would deter the Devil, the **emerald (6)**, in legend a stone fallen from Lucifer's crown, and the **agate (7)**, which folklore said could deflect weapons.

8 PROCESSION

Ritual procession was an ancient tactic to ward off misfortune. Hence the once-common practice of parading around newly sown land with a sanctified object or animal to protect crops from disease – in effect, drawing a symbolic circle around the fields.

9 CRESCENT

The moon goddess Hecate was credited with protecting Byzantium in 341BCE when a crescent moon suddenly broke through clouds above the city as hostile Macedonian forces were approaching it under cover of darkness. Defenders manned the walls and the attack was repelled. To commemorate Hecate, a

See also:

1 Bad Luck, p.77; War and Victory, p.278; Harmony and Meditation, p.290

crescent and star image was stamped on the city's coinage. This decorative device continued to be popular and was adopted centuries later by the Turks and by many subsequent Islamic nations, with protective and other symbolic meanings.

10 HORSESHOE

The protective symbolism of the crescent or horned moon, which appears widely in Egyptian iconography as well as in Islamic art, appears to be the origin of the horseshoe's popularity as a charm against evil and ill fortune. For good luck, the horns must point upward so that the horseshoe forms a containing shape. Britain's Admiral Nelson's ship Victory is said to have sailed into battle with a horseshoe nailed to the mast.

11 CROSS SIGN

Making the sign of the cross by touching the forehead, breast and each shoulder was originally a symbol of Christian faith and a gesture of benediction or conclusion to prayer. But its superstitious use to ward off bad luck or invoke good luck became so popular that the Church, particularly the Protestants, later tried to discourage it. The same gesture was already in use among Jewish worshippers before the birth of Jesus, when it imitated the T-shape of the magnificent temple built 29–9BCE in Jerusalem by Herod the Great.

12 KNOTS

The idea that knots could block evil led to them becoming symbols of protection in Islam, where complex knot designs are sometimes found carved into the walls of palaces. Knotting a beard was thought to frustrate demons. The same symbolism may explain why, in northern Europe, superstitious fishermen used to tie knots in handkerchiefs – apparently to block bad weather.

13 MASKS

Some early cultures appear to have used masks of the animals they hunted in the belief that this would enable them to capture the animals' spirits and prevent harm being caused. Others chose powerful animals as totemic protective symbols and wore imitative masks of them in shamanic ritual and dance to scare off enemies, human or supernatural. The festival masks that are still used in Asian lion and dragon dances have protective rather than aggressive meaning.

Other ways of masking the face or body could also acquire protective symbolism. Hence the aura of the legendary **cloak (14)** that confers invisibility on the heroes of Celtic and Teutonic myths. The nun's **veil (15)** symbolizes protection as well as separation from the ordinary world. The custom of wearing it may derive from the veils worn by consecrated virgins in temples of the ancient world.

16 LANTERN

Associations between light and divinity make any form of lamp or torch symbolically protective. Lanthorns and other enclosed lights had particular emblematic meaning because of their role in combating the perils of the night outdoors. In China, magic lanterns have been used for centuries in festivals to ward off evil spirits of misfortune.

17 WREATH

Wreaths made of sacred plants and worn by rulers were once thought to have protective powers. The emperor Tiberius, who feared death by lightning, is said to have called for his laurel wreath to be brought whenever thunderstorms broke out. Other plants with protective symbolism include **mistletoe (18)**, revered in the Celtic world and mentioned by Virgil as the talisman carried by Aeneas in the underworld, and **elder (19)**, thought to keep witches at bay at times of seasonal changeover when evil abounded. The tradition of touching **wood (20)** derives from ancient cults in which trees were worshipped as protective spirits.

21 EARTH

The protective symbolism of the Earth was virtually universal in ancient cultures. In art, the planet is usually personified by the figure of the **mother (22)** or a woman heavy with child – an emblem of nourishing care.

23 WOMB

The obvious role of the womb as the cradle of life transferred its protective symbolism to a number of containing shapes, in particular to boats such as the biblical **ark**

See also:

16 Masculinity and Virility, p.117

17 War and Victory, p.279

(24). The **coffin (25)** was once a womb symbol associated with rebirth and was therefore constructed with great protective care for the bodies of important people.

26 BELL

The bell is linked in many religions with exorcism or the banishing of evil. Buddhists, Muslims, Hindus and Christians have all taken the sound of a bell symbolically as a divine protective voice.

27–31 BODY

Certain parts of the human body can symbolize protection. This is the defensive meaning of the protruding **tongue (27)** seen in images of the Egyptian god Bes. Other protective divinities, such as the Greek Hermes and the Roman Janus, have multiple **heads (28)** to indicate all-seeing guardianship. The combined female and male heads on some Egyptian statues have similar meaning. In several other cultures, four-headed **tetramorphs (29)** protect the directions of space. The biblical prophet Ezekiel saw such creatures in a vision, with the heads of a man, lion, ox and eagle. The **hand (30)**, with palm open and facing outward, is usually a protective, blocking

See also:

26 Death, p.300
30 Power, p.91;
Charity, Care and
Compassion, p.173

symbol. In some contexts, the **phallus (31)** was a defensive image. Greek and Roman gardeners sometimes used statues of Priapus, the son of Dionysus (Bacchus), to scare birds or other marauders away from their vineyards or orchards with his overscale, red-painted phallus.

32 WINGS

The sheltering symbolism of being taken under somebody's wing is based not only on the mothering habits of birds but on the many winged protective spirits which appear in Middle Eastern art as temple guardians. In Hebrew tradition, the wings of protective **cherubim (33)** form

Jehovah's throne. The **griffin (34)**, a fabulous winged creature melding the powers of lion and eagle, seems to have been a protective emblem in the decoration of Minoan palaces on Crete. The **sphinx (35)**, originally a lion with human or ram head, developed wings as it evolved into the hybrid creature shown in guardian statues of the Middle East and Greece.

36 VULTURE

An unexpected protective emblem is the vulture, which represented the Upper Egyptian goddess Nekbhet as guardian of the pharaoh. The symbolism of the vulture headdress worn by the pharaoh's queen probably derived from this predator's fierce defence of her chicks.

37 COCK

The symbolism of the cock as a protective bird is very ancient, no doubt because its cry announces the return of light after darkness and because it also represents other defensive virtues such as courage and vigilance. Hence the superstition that ghosts fled at cockcrow.

38 LION

The lion is an ambivalent symbol in the West, having both aggressive and defensive associations. But in parts of Asia, lion statues are protective. Hence the chow-faced lions called *karashishi* that guard Buddhist temples in China.

39 RAM

In Christian iconography the ram is usually a protective symbol, particularly when it appears with the figure of Christ. The sacred Hebrew ram's horn called the *shofar* has protective significance when it is blown in religious rituals.

See also:

32 Fame and Fortune, p.70

38 Anger and Cruelty, p.248

40   TIGER

Stone tigers appear on graves and doorways in China as protective emblems, and it was once customary for children to wear tiger caps, with the same defensive significance. In Chinese mythology and art, blue, black, red, white and yellow tigers protect the directions of space – east, north, west, south and the centre.

41   SNAKE

The snake, perhaps the most complex and varied of all animals in its symbolism, often appears in iconography and legend as a protector. The Hindu story of the creator god Vishnu resting on a giant snake's coils is reminiscent of earlier myths of a world snake coiled supportively round the Earth. A cobra with seven hoods is shown guarding the Buddha, and the *naga* (snake) cults common to the great Indian religions have left many protective snake or snake-human carvings on the walls of temples. Snakes entwine the **caduceus (42)**, a decorative rod that was used as a herald's badge of office in the Greco-Roman world. It was thought to have magical power to protect its bearer from being molested in the course of his duties.

See also:

40 Anger and Cruelty, p.248

41 Mortality and Transience, p.35; Evil, p.155; Envy and Jealousy, p.245

The caduceus was sometimes topped with wings to symbolize that it was sacred to Hermes (Mercury), messenger of the gods in classical mythology.

43 RED

As the colour of blood and life, red is sometimes used with protective symbolism. The red beauty spot worn by women in Asia has this meaning.

44 GARLIC

Garlic has had emblematic meaning in Europe for centuries as a plant credited with magical, protective powers. Bunches hung in houses were once thought to deflect the evil eye and to deter lightning, snakes and vampires.

45 SALT

The idea that it is bad luck to spill salt goes back to the classical world in which this invaluable preservative took on wider meaning as an emblem of protection. Leonardo da Vinci appears to have used this traditional symbolism in his famous painting, *The Last Supper* (c.1495). Judas Iscariot is shown spilling the salt.

46 SEVEN

Seven is the most auspicious number, possibly because it was associated with the seven heavenly bodies visible to ancient astronomers and therefore with the deities who were believed to watch over the affairs of human beings. It had protective significance in Arab tradition, particularly for expectant mothers.

47 RUNES

The early Gothic signs known as runes, initially based on classical alphabetic lettering, acquired protective symbolism through associations with Teutonic mythology and magic. The runes some-times found carved on graves seem to be pseudo-magical motifs intended to guard the bodies they contain.

See also:

46 Gluttony, Sloth, Avarice and Pride, p.192

48 TATTOOS

Tattoos often have protective significance for their wearers, especially when they depict powerful beasts or form supposedly magical signs. In tropical jungles, some primitive peoples, like the Dayaks of Borneo, tattooed overall designs which provided the literal protection of camouflage by imitating the colours and forms of the jungle in which they lived and hunted for food.

49 IRON

Because it was associated with early weapons and with fire itself, iron was considered to have protective qualities as well as aggressive ones, and in ancient Egypt it had talismanic value in warding off evil. This may

account for the protective symbolism of **nails (50)** and for curious customs such as the Chinese habit of hammering additional nails into a house post to drive away bad spirits. The Romans ceremoniously drove a nail into a wall of Jupiter's temple each September as insurance against disaster.

See also:

53 Health, p.80; Prudence and Wisdom, p.207; Rebirth and Resurrection, p.333 and p.334

MORTALITY AND TRANSIENCE

51 FATES

The idea that human life has a variable but limited span is personified in a number of legends by the Fates, a group of three crones who spin, measure and cut the thread upon which each individual destiny hangs. In Greek mythology, the best known and probably the most feared of them is Atropos, whose **shears (52)** symbolize mortality. She uses them to sever the thread that is spun by Clotho and measured by Lachesis, the other members of the alarming trio called the Moirai.

53 SNAKE

Blame for the transience of human life is laid on the snake, both in the Bible and in the earlier Babylonian myth of Gilgamesh. The hero of this name sets out to find the magic plant of rejuvenation for humanity and succeeds, only to have it stolen by a snake. In the Bible, Adam and Eve are tempted by a cunning serpent to eat fruit of the "tree of knowledge of good and evil" in defiance of God's wishes and ignoring his warning that death will follow. This blame symbolism is carried through in Christian art, where the snake is sometimes shown at the foot of the Cross as an emblem of the Fall.

54 FLOWERS

Flowers often function as symbols of the human life span and the hope of rebirth, as in the Japanese art of flower decorating called **Ikebana (55)**. Similar themes run through Western poetry and art. In European *vanitas* paintings of the 16th and 17th centuries, the **still life (56)** was used as a poignant reminder of the brevity of life. To symbolize a patron's awareness of the vanity of worldly goods, a mature or **blown rose (57)** might lie among other objects showing off his or her wealth. Other flowers associated with transience include the **anemone (58)**, probably because of its fleeting blossom and its very name, meaning "of the wind".

59 WIND

Wind became a symbol of transience long before Harold Macmillan claimed that the "winds of change" were blowing through Africa or Bob Dylan sang of the answer "blowing in the wind". Artists sometimes suggest mortality in landscapes by showing wind-drifted leaves or bare trees swaying.

See also:

54 Longevity, p.42; Fertility, p.53

63 Protection, p.24; Masculinity and Virility, p.117

60 **TIME**

Symbols of time appear in many devotional paintings to indicate the inexorable passage of life. They include the **hour glass (61)** which is often shown as an attribute of Father Time and of Death personified. Its flowing sand provides a striking image of the escaping years. In still life art, a **clock (62)** usually has the same symbolism.

63 **CANDLE**

The guttering candle is another symbol of mortality often seen in still life paintings. Its short life and easily extinguished flame make the analogy obvious. Psychologically, the tradition of blowing out candles on birthday cakes, offers an intriguing reverse symbolism: the past years are extinguished but the vital breath of life demonstrates that future years lie ahead.

64 **CUP**

The cup, like the candle, is one of a number of symbols that can have reverse symbolism. As a containing form, it suggests life; overturned, it suggests emptiness, and therefore the vanity of life.

Shown tipped over on a table or ledge, the empty cup was a popular way for painters to demonstrate their technical virtuosity while at the same time making a symbolic point.

65 SKULL

Hans Holbein the Younger, an artist obsessed with mortality, used a skull in his famous 1533 painting *The Ambassadors* to undermine the impression of confidence given by the two men who are posed, together with instruments of science, in the double portrait. The skull lies on the floor at their feet, its form concealed by skilful perspective distortion unless viewed from the right angle. The intention is a *memento mori* pointing out the vanity of earthly achievements. Skulls frequently appear in portraits of saints to symbolize the religious thinker's constant awareness of the transience of all material things.

66 BUBBLE

Paintings in which chubby and angelic figures known as *putti* (little boys) are seen blowing bubbles are allegories of mortality. Buddhism also uses the bubble as a symbol of the transience of earthly life.

LONGEVITY

67 TREES

The strength, toughness and durability of certain trees made them apt symbols of long life, particularly among the Chinese, for whom longevity was regarded as one of the greatest of all human blessings. The solitary towering **pine (68)** often has this meaning in both Chinese and Japanese paintings. **Fruit trees (69)** are also popular oriental emblems of long life, especially the pear, peach, apple and plum. In Western tradition, a different species of pine, the **cedar (70)**, has a pre-eminent place, particularly in the Near and Middle East. Its heartwood was used in statuary and sacred architecture, and Celtic embalmers used its resin, perhaps because of its association with longevity. Some North American tribes associated the branching antlers of the **stag (71)** with trees and, through their seasonal shedding and regrowth, with both longevity and rebirth.

72 MUSHROOMS

Mushrooms are unexpected symbols of long life in China, possibly because the hallucinogenic effect of eating certain species linked them with magical powers. In Chinese legend, mushrooms were believed to be the food of the Immortals.

73–4 MIGRATING BIRDS

The impressive seasonal reappearances of some large migrating birds made them symbols of longevity in Chinese and Japanese traditions. Both the **stork (73)** and the **crane (74)** are shown with this symbolic meaning in Oriental art.

75 TURTLE

The primordial turtle is an image of unchanging stability in Chinese mythology. Apart from their ancient appearance, turtles must have often been seen outliving successive generations of human owners. They are the world's longest-lived vertebrates and are remarkably durable, often surviving for weeks without food – life spans of well over 200 years are possible. Turtles or tortoises have been kept as pets in China for centuries, and familiarity with them has justifiably made them popular symbols of longevity.

See also:

73 Fecundity and Plenty, p.59

74 Fidelity and Loyalty, p.214

76 CHRYSANTHEMUM

Another Eastern emblem of longevity is the chrysanthemum – the flower of the imperial family in Japan. This symbolism may be linked with the flower's ability to blossom in late autumn or early winter.

77 THISTLE

Thistles also appear in the long catalogue of Eastern longevity symbols. In addition to their defensive capacities and hardiness, they are exceptionally tenacious plants when used for decorative purposes and will long hold their general form after having been cut.

78 RUBY

Among stones, the ruby is most often used as a symbol of longevity in Indian and Burmese traditions. Apart from its hardness, its colour suggests life.

79 GREEN

The word "evergreen" is almost a synonym for continuing vitality. Green has particular emblematic importance in China, partly through its connection with spring but also through the positive symbolism of jade, which is associated with longevity as well as with the hope of rebirth.

FERTILITY

80   MOTHER

The very wide range of symbols used to invoke successful childbirth or celebrate the continuity of human life demonstrates the fundamental importance of fertility in ancient cultures. The most obvious of these symbols is the mother. Throughout Europe, archaeologists have found figurines carved from small stones dating back to the upper Paleolithic period, some 30,000 years ago – the earliest works that can be called art. Their swelling breasts and bellies, sometimes representational, sometimes shown as abstract forms, personify the concept of fertility. Small statuettes, such as the famous "Venus of Willendorf" discovered in Austria, may have been held in the hand as amulets. Larger stones, with

See also:

79 Envy and Jealousy, p.246

shapes suggesting the maternal figure, were later
worshipped as mother goddesses.

81 MOON

With its constantly changing form and its apparent cyclic
death, rebirth and growth, the moon was once not only
thought to control the rhythms of women's menstrual cycles
but also to play a vital role in the germination of plant, animal and human life. The **harvest moon (82)**, a full moon
near the September equinox in the Northern Hemisphere,
has been linked with love and fertility for centuries.
Agricultural and human fertility is the underlying symbolism
of the moon festival, still held at this time in China.

83 LOZENGE

Fertility was sometimes represented in the abstract form
of the lozenge, a diamond-shaped ideogram of the vulva.
Lozenges appear with fertility symbolism on the jade skirt
of the Mexican nature goddess Chalchiuhtlicue,
for example. Christian painters and sculptors may
have taken over and sanctified the ancient fertility
symbolism of the lozenge by depicting the Virgin
Mary enclosed in the less angular lozenge form
known in art as the mandorla.

See also:

81 Beauty and
Grace, p.131;
Immortality and
Eternity, p.326

84 PHALLUS

The phallus was widely connected with spring fertility rites, sometimes taking the symbolic form of a stone column or wooden pole. The English tradition of dancing round a **maypole (85)** is a relic of ancient festivals invoking both agricultural and human fruitfulness. This May Day custom was condemned by the Puritans in the 17th century for encouraging "raging fleshly lusts". Another fertility symbol substituting for the phallus is the **tongue (86)**, often shown protruding and exaggerated in size in tribal art. Extended tongues on statues do not always symbolize fertility, but Dyak "pole figures" of Borneo do have this emblematic meaning.

87 ANIMALS

In ritual magic, and in art, animals were the most common symbols of fertility. The legendary potency of **bulls (88)** is invoked in thousands of ancient images beginning with the huge beasts stampeding across the walls of caves such as those at Lascaux in France or Altamira in Spain. The 1st-century Greek historian Diodorus Siculus describes Egyptian women exposing themselves to the bull god Apis in fertility rites. Bull sacrifices in the Mithraic rites of Persia mimed the slaughter of a primordial bull whose prolific semen fertilized the whole world.

The **horse (89)**, which has a wide range of different symbolic associations, also had a place in fertility ritual. Autumnal sacrifices to Mars, Roman god of agriculture as well as war, involved a horse whose tail was kept throughout the winter as an emblem of spring fertility. Agricultural or human fertility was a central element in early cults of the **snake (90)**, and may explain why snakes were carved into palaeolithic antlers or inscribed on rock faces. Links with the umbilical cord and penis make

See also:

87 War and Victory, p.277; Death, p.299

the sexual symbolism of the snake feminine as well as masculine, and a snake wound round a tree is a specific symbol of Ishtar, the greatest fertility goddess of the Middle East. Followers of another fertility deity of Asia Minor, Sabazius, mimed the passage of a snake through the body of each new cult member. By visual analogy, the snake was also linked with lightning and its fertilizing powers. In countries of the Pacific, where snakes were unknown, the **eel (91)** replaces it as a phallic fertility symbol.

Antlers (92) worn by shamans or gods in early art appear to be emblems of fertility, as in images of the Celtic god Cernunnos, who is specifically linked with crop growth. This symbolism is continued in antlered or horned animals such as the **stag (93)** and the **ram (94)**. Hence, perhaps, the choice of the ram, Aries, as the first sign of the zodiac, symbolizing the strengthening of the sun at the March equinox and the return of spring fertility. Not surprisingly, some prolific breeders appear as fertility emblems, notably the **rabbit (95)** and **hare (96)**. Their symbolism is difficult to separate, and both were used as charms against sterility or to encourage pregnancy and ease childbirth. Pliny mentions use of a rabbit's foot as sympathetic magic, and the "Easter Bunny" is linked to spring fertility, a reference to the hare-headed Anglo-Saxon fertility goddess, Eostre. The prolific spawn issued by **fish (97)** led to sexual associations between them, the penis and sperm, which resulted in fish becoming emblems of fertility and fecundity also.

98 WATER

Water and, by extension, the natural forces associated with it, such as **thunder (99)**, **lightning (100)** and **rain (101)**, together with **springs (102)** and the **sea (103)**, all have fertility symbolism and are often personified by major gods or goddesses. Virtually all cosmologies associate the origin and continuance of life with water, an element invariably feminine in symbolism. The link between lightning and impregnation can be seen in Aboriginal art where lightning is represented as a cosmic erect penis. The fertilizing downpour storms release was symbolized in Central America by an ideogram somewhat like a comb, the teeth representing falling rain. This is the attribute in Aztec art of Tlaloc (the Mayan Chak), supreme fertility god. Springs, fountains, lakes and wells often had sacred significance as sources of life. The sea itself is the original source of life in many ancient traditions – a maternal image even more primary than the earth.

104 RICE

The custom of scattering confetti over a bridal couple appears to have been taken from India where rice was used in Hindu wedding ceremonials as a symbol of fertility as well as prosperity.

105 CORN

Cereal plants of several kinds were used as fertility emblems in many ancient traditions. Female icons made out of maize stalks had this significance among tribes in Peru as well as North America.

106 FRUIT

Certain fruits had strong fertility symbolism and can appear with this meaning in art. The **apple (107)** is a famous example, its sexual symbolism perhaps based on the vulva-like shape of its core in cross-section. Another is the **pomegranate (108)**, which the Romans called the "apple of Carthage". In the Mediterranean world, the numerous seeds within the juicy pulp suggested many children, and the same symbolism led to the pomegranate becoming one of the "Three Blessed Fruits" in Chinese Buddhist traditions.

109 TREES

The fruitfulness of trees and their phallic symbolism led to them becoming the focal point of ancient fertility rites in many parts of the early world. In his book *The Golden Bough*, J.G. Frazer claimed that in Asia the links between the fertility of trees and humans were so strong that blossoming fruit trees were treated with as much care and consideration as a pregnant woman. Folk customs in which barren women embraced certain trees or lay beneath them in order to become pregnant are known from areas as widespread as northwestern Europe and Polynesia.

In the early civilization of Mesopotamia, masculine generative force was symbolized by phallic shape of the **pine cone (110)**, which is depicted in art as an emblem of the hero-god Marduk. As fruit of the Druidic oak, the **acorn (111)** also had procreative symbolism. Visual associations between it and the head of the penis may account for its appearance in some Celtic carvings.

112 MISTLETOE

Because it produces yellow flowers and white berries in the middle of winter, mistletoe was taken by the ancients and used as a symbol of fertility and potency, particularly when it was found clinging to oak trees. The Druids gave it feminine-masculine meaning, the juice of the berries being emblematic of semen. These ancient Celtic associations with fertility are the probable origin of the modern Christmas custom of kissing under a bunch of mistletoe.

113 FLOWERS

The receptacle shape of flowers means that they are generally feminine in symbolism and their unfurling is sometimes associated with birthing. Among the Aztecs, the flower goddess Xochiquetzal was specifically a fertility deity and is said to have been the first woman to give birth to twins.

The sexual symbolism of the **lotus (114)** made it the flower that was most often associated with child-bearing. The lotus is one of the Buddhist "Eight Auspicious Signs" in China, where the blessing of many children is represented by the image of a boy holding a lotus. Another Chinese floral emblem of fertility is the magnificent cup-shaped

orchid (115), which was once believed to be a charm against sterility.

In Japan, the distinctly feminine **peony (116)** was a popular bridal flower auguring a fruitful union. However, in pre-Christian art the **lily (117)** had male fertility symbolism through its phallic-shaped pistil, and it often appears as a decorative motif in the Greek world, perhaps with this sub-text.

118 SPIRAL

Spiral forms are found worldwide as decorative motifs and in some cases are fertility emblems. This is particularly true of the double spiral which can be read as a combined male-female image – the unfurling penis and the involuted birth canal. In both South East Asia and Polynesia, spiral body and face tattoos often had sexual symbolism based on the forms of unfolding ferns or other forest plants.

119 EMERALD

The emerald is often associated with fertility, probably due to the fact that its green hue suggests growth and spring germination. It acquired folk symbolism as

a lucky stone of conception and childbirth and was believed
to shorten labour.

120 PEARL

A number of symbolic associations make the pearl a powerful fertility emblem – its links with water, its secret growth
inside a shell (a vulva and womb symbol) and its pale luminosity which resembles trapped moonlight (also suggestive
of fertility cycles). In classical tradition, the pearl was the
stone worn by Aphrodite, the fertility goddess known to the
Babylonians as Ishtar and to the Romans as Venus.

121 SCEPTRE

The sceptre, often carried by rulers, is a fertility as well as
a power emblem, its symbolism derived from the virility
and masculinity associations of the rod or staff. Some
sceptres are also linked to the germinating force of the
thunderbolt, in particular the Tibetan *dorje* and the Hindu
and Buddhist diamond sceptre, or *vajra*, although these also
have spiritual meaning.

FECUNDITY AND PLENTY

122 EARTH

Many fertility symbols represent the fecundity of nature rather than of humans, although the two ideas are so closely interlinked that it is often hard to disentangle them. An example is the earth itself, which is almost everywhere personified as both womanly and fecund, as in the classical Gaia, the goddess that gives birth to life in the Greek pantheon. The male Egyptian earth god, Geb, is a notable exception. The masculine role in earth fertility symbolism was sometimes played by the **plough (123)**, hence the Chinese custom whereby a new emperor was required to demonstrate his responsibility for his country's fertility by carrying out a little emblematic ploughing. **Soil (124)** was sometimes used in rites of passage as a fertility emblem, and the sympathetic magic of burial and "rebirth" could also be used as a fertility ritual. Echoes of these ancient

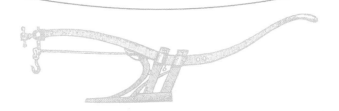

practices survived until relatively recent times in some rural communities where coupling in newly-ploughed furrows was a popular custom at spring fertility festivals. The germinating spirits of the earth were often thought to be concentrated in **caves (125)**, which had widespread womb symbolism. **Dwarfs (126)** have always traditionally been associated with caves and with knowledge of the natural powers of the earth. This could explain why some fertility gods of Mexico were dwarfs, and why the garden gnome's popularity has never faded.

127 GARDEN

The garden is a powerful symbol of both fecundity and fertility, and appears with this meaning in many paintings. Christian artists often placed the Virgin Mary within a walled garden which functioned as an emblem of the Madonna's sealed fruitfulness.

128 MILK

Few cultures do not give milk a primary place as a symbol of fecundity and plenty. It was poured on the ground in the Egyptian rites of Osiris, god of fertility as well as of the underworld. It

See also:

125 Enlightenment and Transformation, pp.343–4

was similarly used elsewhere as a spring libation to promote crop growth. **Breasts (129)** have the same symbolism in images of fertility goddesses who are sometimes shown multi-breasted or with unusually large breasts, as in the Venus of Willendorf.

130 CLOUDS

Dense, heavy clouds of the cumulonimbus type had inevitable fecundity symbolism for agrarian communities waiting for drought to break. Swelling cloud forms sometimes appear in North American Indian paintings designed to invoke rain.

131 FROG

Heket, the Egyptian frog goddess of birth, personified the fetal symbolism of the frog and its association with germination, fecundity, rain and water which made it an emblem of fertility in many other cultures. The Chinese and Peruvians were among several peoples who used frog images to call up rain showers, sometimes by the use of items with frog motifs. Frogs also feature in some Navajo sand paintings, probably with the same intention.

132   STORK

The fecundity symbolism of the stork flying in with new-born babies, a tale told to children by generations of expectant mothers, seems to have originated in Greece where the bird was sometimes linked with the birth goddess Hera (Juno to the Romans), protector of women.

133   COW

The fecundity of the cow and its plentiful milk gave it mothering and nourishing symbolism across Europe and Asia in ritual, religion, legend and art. The Egyptian mother goddess Hathor, nourisher of all life, is represented as a cow and so, sometimes, is the sky goddess Nut, who appears as a cow with stars on her belly. Greek myth said that milk from the breast of Hera, originally also a cow goddess, was so abundant that it formed the Milky Way when she was suckling Herakles and he tugged too hard.

134 SOW

The sow was another Great Mother emblem of fecundity, sometimes appearing as an alternative to the cow in Egyptian and Greek mythology and art. In the Celtic world, abundance was personified by the sow goddess Ceridwen. Pigs were often sacrificed to agricultural deities as fertility emblems in Greece and Italy.

135 GOAT

The female goat, whose milk is suitable for human babies, is the other animal most often used as an emblem of fecundity and nourishment. In Greek myth, the great god Zeus himself

was suckled by the goat Amalthea. The story that he accidentally broke off one of her horns, which proved to have the magical property of providing limitless nourishment, gave rise to the emblem of abundance most popular with Western artists, the **cornucopia (136)**. This "horn of plenty"

appears brimming with fruits and grains in numerous paintings based on classical mythology, often, but not always, portraying vegetation or wine divinities. It derives from even more ancient traditions of the horn as a male fertility symbol.

137   TREES

Food-bearing trees were often venerated in early times as embodiments of nourishing Earth Mother goddesses. One tree with particularly widespread fecundity symbolism is the **fig (138)**. For some Middle-Eastern peoples, it was so important as a source of food that it was worshipped as the Tree of Life, particularly in Egypt where the tree was sacred

See also:

135 Masculinity and Virility, p.121; Lust, p.241; Purification, Atonement and Propitiation, p.365

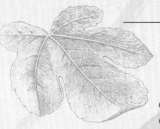

to the mother and sky goddesses Hathor and Nut.

Further south in Africa, the folklore of Chad said that sterility would fall on anyone who attempted to prune the tree. In Islamic tradition, the fig appears as the tree of utmost desire, forbidden to touch in paradise. India linked it with the procreative power of Shiva and Vishnu. This sexual symbolism arises from its milky juice and from the suggestive shape that made its leaf famous as a cover for the male genitalia. The **banyan (139)** species of fig, with its proliferating aerial roots, is a sacred symbol of fecundity in India. The symbolism of plenty is continued in Roman tradition, where the fig is the tree under which Romulus and Remus were suckled and an attribute of the vegetation god Bacchus.

The **olive (140)** was also revered for its reliability as a food source. The patronage of Athens was said to have been awarded to Athene because she gave the tree to the city. The bounty of the **date palm (141)**, essentially a masculine symbol in the Middle East, made it the Tree of Life in Arabia, and it also had female fecundity symbolism in China.

142 GRAPEVINE

The vine has become, in religion, myth and art,
almost a summary of fecundity and providential
nourishment. Dating far back in Middle-Eastern
traditions, it has this symbolic meaning in the Old
Testament where it is an emblem of God's blessing
on his chosen people. It is also linked as an
emblem of fertility with ancient agricultural gods
of Mesopotamia as well as the classical Dionysus and
Bacchus. The same symbolism appears in Egyptian art
where vinous motifs are associated with the
vegetation god Osiris.

143 BEANS

Like other multi-seeded foods, including pomegranates,
beans had fecundity symbolism in some cultures, which is
why they came to have male sexual significance and were
used as folk charms in Japan and India. In Japan they were
often scattered throughout houses in order to ward off
lightning and evil spirits.

WEALTH AND PROSPERITY

144 PROSPERITY GODS

Personifications of wealth and prosperity are far more prevalent in Asian iconography than in Western. European artists enjoyed painting elaborate displays of wealth, but the symbolic message was that it denoted, at best, vanity and, at worst, avarice. By contrast, a host of minor Asian deities appear in statuary to proclaim prosperity as a blessing.

Images of the ample Indonesian prosperity god **Jambhala (145)** were probably used to invoke windfalls. He is shown sitting on a cushion as well-rounded as his own stomach. The **pot belly (146)** is usually an emblem of prosperity in Eastern art, which is how the important Japanese rice god **Inari (147)**, also a prosperity god in the Japanese pantheon, is depicted, as is **Daikoku (148)**. Both are often shown accompanied by a **rat (149)** which, by association with its ability to find its way into rice granaries, is an emblem of riches. Unlike its negative Western symbolism, the rat's reputation as an ingenious food provider made it an exemplary animal in Asia. South Chinese legend credited it with discovering rice for humankind.

150 EGG

The propitious symbolism of the egg appears in countless folk tales throughout the world and is often connected with the arrival of unexpected wealth. This emblematic meaning can

probably be explained by the golden yolk concealed within the blank shell. Some of the egg's cosmic symbolism also links with prosperity – the gold sun and silver moon. Fairytale gooses lay golden eggs, dragons guard them, and Laotian folklore says that prosperity is symbolized by dreams in which a hen lays many eggs.

151 FISH

Fish also appear in folklore as emblems of prosperity, especially in China. Their prolific spawn and fecundity symbolism may account for this, but in some tales they rise to the surface of the water carrying in their mouths lost treasures from the deep.

152 SHELLS

Like many fertility emblems, shells are linked with prosperity as well as sexual happiness. And for some tribes of the Pacific their value was literal. The **cowrie (153)**, sometimes golden in hue, was prized and traded both there and in parts of Africa.

154 METALS AND PRECIOUS STONES

Some things transcend their own value to become general symbols of wealth. This is true of **gold (155)**, particularly in its emblematic use invoking the sun in statuary, decorative art and costume. Cleopatra is said to have dropped a **pearl (156)** into her wine glass and swallowed it during a banquet with Mark Antony in order to demonstrate how rich she was. Other stones, such as the **agate (157)** were thought to bring their owners prosperity and were worn as lucky charms for this reason.

158   RAINBOW

Legends of the "pot of gold" at the end of the rainbow draw on ancient links between prosperity and the fertilizing forces of sun and rain. Connecting the spiritual and material planes of sky and earth, rainbows were thought to have the power to offer magical (but always elusive) treasures to those who chased them.

159   SPIDER

In folklore, spiders presage rain or wealth to come, and it is bad luck to harm them. The symbolic analogy is between the spider descending its thread and ancient beliefs or hopes that heavenly gifts would be showered from above upon the deserving.

Domesticated animals became obvious symbols of prosperity in early herding societies where, as the Bible demonstrates, wealth was counted in numbers of sheep, goats, camels or other creatures. The **calf (161)** could symbolize prosperity, as in the story of the Prodigal Son for whom a fatted calf was killed. The biblical Golden Calf is also taken as an emblem of material wealth (damned in this case for religious reasons). For the Plains Indians of North America, the ancient symbol of prosperity was the **buffalo (162)**, a vital resource for its flesh, bones, skin, fat, tendons and horn. Before their virtual annihilation by settlers, buffalo proliferated in their millions in the region's vast prairies.

Some wild animals, however, had emblematic associations based more on links they were supposed to have with beneficial spirits or good fairies. A famous example is the **reindeer (163)**. It became the traditional hauler of Santa's gift-laden sleigh not only because it inhabited the snowy, Christmassy wastes of the north, but also because in Celtic folklore, deer were herded by fairies. Their **antlers (164)** had much earlier symbolic links with prosperity. Antlered divinities

represented growth, spring fertility
and, by extension, wealth.

The **elephant (165)** is
an ancient symbol of prosperity in India, where to
own one was a mark of
wealth. Several stories
account for the contrary modern
symbolism of the "white elephant", which
refers to an unwanted possession. One is that
the circus entrepreneur P.T. Barnum bought a rare white
elephant that did not recover its very high purchase cost.

166 CUCKOO

In European folklore, the call of the cuckoo in springtime
presaged riches. Curious superstitions attached themselves
to this notion. In France, it was considered lucky to have
coins in your pockets when the call was heard. In the Alps,
rattling or turning the coins while the cuckoo called was said
to ensure that family funds would not run out during the
next hard winter. The cuckoo's prosperity symbolism may
have arisen from songs and poems in which this bird was
the harbinger of spring fertility, or simply from its repetitive
call, prompting the wishful idea of coins being multiplied.

FAME AND FORTUNE

167 WINGS

Fame was a popular subject for Western artists and their patrons, and was personified at first by various classical figures equipped with the symbolic wings of ascension. These included the Roman divinity **Mercury (168)** who, as the fleet-footed herald of the gods, had the ability to spread renown around the world. Alternatively, Fame is represented by the legendary winged horse **Pegasus (169)**, or by a winged female figure bearing aloft the glorious dead.

170 TRUMPET

The ringing notes of the trumpet, first used
by the Romans to announce cavalry charges,
became the herald of other significant events
and eventually made the instrument an emblem of importance in general. Hence it became the main attribute of
Fame personified in Renaissance painting. Bernardo Strozzi,
the Genoese painter of the early 17th century, depicted
the female figure of Fame holding a trumpet. The origin
of the phrase "blowing his own trumpet" is thought to have
come from medieval jousting, in which trumpets announced
each contestant.

71–2 FORTUNE

Fortune, in the sense of good luck, is not a concept often
portrayed in Western art, as its two best-known personifications demonstrate. The Roman goddess **Fortuna (171)** is
more often a symbolic reminder that good fortune may not
last. Some paintings show her with a cornucopia of good
things. But she was associated by several classical writers
with the sea and its inconstant moods. This led to her being
depicted in Renaissance paintings with nautical attributes –
ship, rudder, billowing sail – and standing on a globe. A
still more unreliable figure is **Dame Fortune (172)**, whose

attribute is a wheel. A popular image in medieval art, particularly in Spain, was of this fateful woman turning a wheel that carried some up and cast others down.

173 GODS OF HAPPINESS

Good luck divinities were turned into popular amulets in both China and Japan. In China, they are represented as five old men symbolizing the blessings of health, wealth, virtue, long life and natural death. Their attributes shown in art differ but often include **bats (174)**, a name in China that sounds the same as luck. This explains the otherwise puzzling appearance of five bats on Chinese greeting cards. In Japan, the gods of happiness number seven. They signify guardianship, scholarship, nutrition, fishing, longevity, music and mirth.

175 NUMBERS

Numbers had powerful symbolic meanings in the ancient world as the keys not only to cosmic order under a divine hand but to magical forces that could influence the course of human life. The idea of a personal lucky number is therefore very old. In number symbolism generally, **three (176)** most usually represents good fortune. The fact that if two people cannot agree what to do, a third may break the deadlock is the likely origin of the expression "third time lucky". In action, three suggests decision, hence its association with success. In legends and fairytales, heroes and heroines overcome difficulties at the third try, and are offered three choices or set three tests. And in ritual, many actions are performed three times, as in Islamic custom. Folk superstitions in England recommended turning around three times before making a wish. Three is represented graphically by the triangle.

As the double of three, **six (177)** can also represent luck, as it did in the mathematical system of Pythagoras. But here, luck means chance – the six faces of dice and the swings of fortune predicted in the Chinese system of hexagrams. Good fortune itself is more often associated in China with **eight (178)**, a number which is associated with positive meanings in Buddhism and Taoism, as well as in Japanese Shintoism.

179 CAUL

The caul or uterine membrane that partly covers the heads of some new-born babies was an ancient augury of good luck among Slavic tribes according to Roman writers. It had protective symbolism, specifically against death by drowning.

See also:

175 Bad Luck, pp.76–7; Truth and Deceit, p.170; Prudence and Wisdom, p.210

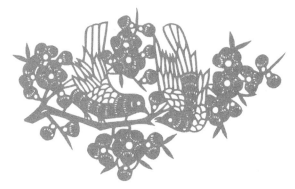

180 MAGPIE

Although the parasitic European species of this bird has negative symbolism, the magpie often appears on Chinese greeting cards as an emblem of luck or good news. In folklore, its call was believed to announce the arrival of friends.

181 ALBATROSS

This large, wandering sea bird's habit of following ships on long voyages gave rise to an old maritime superstition that it was an omen of good luck. Samuel Taylor Coleridge (1772–1834) relied on this symbolism in his famous poem *The Rime of the Ancient Mariner*, in which the bird appears as the saviour of a boat that has been trapped in polar ice. The albatross is, however, finally killed by one of the sailors, with grievous consequences.

182   DEVIL

The arrival of sudden material wealth was regarded with distrust in medieval times, leading to the idea that somebody with an inexplicable run of good fortune might have had supernatural support from the Devil in exchange for his or her soul – hence the old saying, the "luck of the Devil".

183   ORANGES

Oranges are good luck emblems in China, where they are the traditional fruit eaten on the second day of the Chinese New Year. They have ancient associations with luxury and, because of their solar hue, may have been the "golden apples" of Greek myth, guarded by a dragon on the paradisial Islands of the Blessed.

184   RED

Red is one of the most positive of all colours in symbolism because of its associations with festivity, vitality and life itself. Red is representative of luck in China, where it was the emblematic colour of the Chou dynasty (c.1045–256 BCE).

See also:
182 Evil, pp.152–5
184 Protection, p.32

BAD LUCK

185 THIRTEEN

Numerical symbolism originated in the ancient world and is sometimes linked with cosmology and calendrical science. This seems to be true of the number 13, which in Europe has been associated with bad luck for centuries. Its unpopularity is thought to date from problems experienced when some early lunar calendars used a 13th "non-month" to make up the gap between the solar year and 12 phases of the moon. The suggestion is that the number 13 then came to be thought of as unfavourable. In classical times, farmers were advised not to plant on the 13th day. Satan was said to be the 13th figure at witch's rites, and Death is the 13th card of the *major arcana* in the Tarot.

The curious idea that 13 is an unlucky number at a table may derive from the Last Supper (Christ and the 12 disciples). Christ's crucifixion on a Friday certainly explains why

Friday the 13th is considered ominous. Interestingly, in Central America the Mayan calendar, which was solar and based on 20 months, left **five (186)** as the unlucky number, and 13 had positive symbolism as the number of days in each religious week.

187 BLACK

Black day, black mark and black magic are among a host of expressions in which the word black is used almost as a synonym for misfortune or harm. Its colour symbolism derives from the ancient black-white dichotomy in which goodness was associated with light and evil with darkness. Black is usually, but not always, emblematically negative.

Until modern times, this prejudice was sufficient to make the **black cat (188)** an omen of bad luck in folklore and superstition – in medieval times, it was believed to be a witch's familiar, if not an actual incarnation of Satan himself. It was associated with evil in the Celtic world as well as in Islam. Japanese folk tales tell of black cats taking over women's bodies.

189 CROW

The carrion-feeding habits of the European crow, combined with the negative symbolism of black, made it a bird of ill omen which was sometimes associated with death, war, solitude and evil. It is endowed with similarly negative meaning in India. However, the grain-eating species has dramatically different symbolism, especially in North American Indian tradition, where it appears positively as a solar bird, as it also does in China.

190 LEFT SIDE

Roman augurers using the flight of birds to predict future events took their arrival from the left side as an omen of ill fortune. The Latin word for the left side is *sinister*. This link with bad luck, or even evil, undoubtedly influenced Christian symbolism to some degree. Witchcraft associates the left hand with black magic and the right hand with white magic.

See also:

189 War and Victory (Predators), pp.274–5

191 Goodness and Benevolent Power, p.147; Divination, p.373

191   BROKEN MIRROR

The belief that it is bad luck to break a mirror is a superstition backed by a long history of fears primitive peoples have had about reflected images. The image in the glass was thought to share the essence of the person it reflected, representing, in effect, a twin soul that would be lost or harmed if the mirror was damaged. Alfred Lord Tennyson's poem *The Lady of Shallot* (1832) drew on the symbolism of earlier legends in which cracking a magical mirror presaged death.

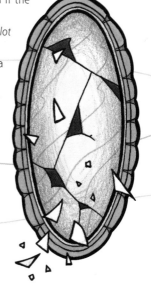

Many other stories feature wizards or sorceresses whose mirrors show impending misfortunes, as Merlin's did. Bad-luck superstitions attach themselves to other broken objects, including necklaces of **pearl (192)**. Here, the symbolism is taken from analogies between pearls and tears, which is why the pearl ring is traditionally considered to be an unlucky wedding jewel.

193–6   HOMEOPATHIC SYMBOLS

A number of creatures with sharply diverging symbolism have homeopathic (in the sense of the "disease that cures") links with medicine. The Swiss psychologist Carl Jung interpreted the **caduceus (193)** as a symbol of this method of healing. An image of two snakes wound round a rod, the caduceus was originally a herald's protective badge of office, but later became an emblem of medicine, and is still used as such today. In form it bears a close resemblance to early Greek images of the staff carried by Aesculapius (a rod entwined by a single snake), the son of Apollo and Greek god of healing and medicine.

Both emblems demonstrate the potent symbolism of the **snake (194)**. Its ancient associations with healing powers, and therefore with Aesculapius, may have been based on its ability to slough off its old skin. When asked for their help in 293BCE when Rome was in the grip of pestilence, the Greeks sent the Romans a sacred snake, claiming

that it incarnated the
spirit of Aesculapius.

This echoes the Old Testament
story of God turning the rod of Moses
into a snake which produces first a
disease and then the cure.

See also:

194 Evil, p.155;
Envy and
Jealousy p.245
196 Evil, p.159

The **scorpion (195)** also had wounding and healing symbolism, suggesting a link with homeopathy – at least among some African tribes. This arose from the idea that it secreted an oily antidote to its venomous sting. For similar reasons, Chinese doctors once used the toxic secretions of the **toad (196)**, an amphibian widely credited with magical powers. Dried toads were still being used as amulets in England during the Great Plague of 1563, when the prominent surgeon Dr George Thomson claimed to have cured himself by using one to absorb the "putrefactive ferment".

197   ANT

Sympathetic magic was a fundamental basis for many primitive cures. It was believed that the power of symbolism could be used to change a patient's psychological outlook. A curious example in North Africa was the feeding of ants to listless people in the belief that the insect's restless activity would transfer itself to their metabolism.

198 UNICORN

The healing reputation of this fabulous beast in Persia was mentioned by the 4th-century BCE Greek physician Ctesias. When the unicorn became a popular decorative motif for medieval Christian artists, its ancient symbolism reappeared in a legend that poisoned water could be purified by a unicorn tracing a cross in it with its horn. The medicinal use of powdered rhinoceros horn in Asia since ancient times probably provides the tenuous link between such stories and reality.

199 STONES AND OTHER AMULETS

Ancient belief in the magical powers of stone, combined with its often suggestive shapes, led to it being used in amulets thought to cure conditions such as impotence and sterility. With its symbolism of durability, **jade (200)** was administered in powdered form to prolong life in China. And because jade stones were often kidney-shaped, they began to be used as a Spanish remedy for kidney disease. The **ruby (201)**, through its blood and vitality symbolism, is a jewel that was once believed to restore the spirits and compensate for loss of blood. Other precious stones with curative symbolism include the **diamond (202)** and the **pearl (203)**, which is still used in powdered form in India. A Roman superstition said the pearl could restore the wits of lunatics.

Wider curative powers were ascribed to the **emerald (204)**, a healing amulet drawing on fertility and occult symbolism. As wizards used it to see into the future, the emerald was thought to improve eyesight. Reputedly, it also shortened labour in childbirth, and prevented dysentry and epileptic fits.

Two stone-like materials were credited with curative properties because of their links to water and its healing symbolism. **Ivory (205)** powdered from walrus tusks, was used in China as an antidote to poison. **Coral (206)**, in its red, Mediterranean hue, was popular with Roman matrons as a means of stemming bleeding and preventing childhood illnesses. It seems to have acquired this significance because red coral was said in classical mythology to have grown from the blood of the sorceress Medusa. Coral necklaces were still being worn as talismans by children in medieval times. Amulets made from the fossil resin, **amber (207)** had equally wide curative symbolism in the classical world, being thought to help gastric problems as well as headaches, rheumatism and asthma.

208 WATER

In addition to its uses as an essential restorative in many medical conditions, pure water, especially rainwater, had considerable symbolic value as a curative, through its ancient links with purification, heavenly blessings and spiritual refreshment.

209 PLANTS

A vast number of plants, particularly herbs, were used in the ancient world in the prevention or treatment of illness, with varying efficacy. Some had symbolic meanings in addition to any curative function. An example is the **mandrake (210)**, Shakespeare's "mandoraga". This Mediterranean plant of the potato family was long used in the ancient world as an emetic, purgative and, most importantly, in medicine as an anti-spasmodic and narcotic. Symbolic values drawn from a resemblance between its forked root and the human form then expanded its supposed benefits to magical powers of facilitating pregnancy.

The medical reputation of **mistletoe (211)**, thought by the Celts to be a cure for sterility as well as an antidote to poison, is also based on its supposed magical and fertilizing powers. Classical myths of Apollo in his role as Paeon, the Healer, bestowed semi-magical status on the **peony (212)**, a flower named for the god. Its roots, seeds and flowers had medicinal uses that were still thought effective in England in the 17th century. The **laurel (213)**, also associated with Apollo, was chewed by the Greeks to combat pestilence. Another flower, the **asphodel (214)**, was associated with the underworld in classical mythology, and its use as an antidote to snakebite was probably based on the snake's own fame as a creature who was at home in the underworld.

Human Qualities and Powers

Power 88

Authority 96

Sovereignty 102

Strength and Stability 108

Masculinity and Virility 114

Femininity and Maternity . . . 122

Beauty and Grace 130

Knowledge and Learning 134

Vigilance and Guardianship . . 138

POWER

215 WHEEL

In the ancient world, the
wheel was a forceful image
of the energy that drives the
cosmos. It became a symbol
of power in the 2nd millennium BCE, when chariot-riding
warriors put wheels to military
use, crushing all before them as
they spread out across Europe. Both
the early solid wheel in the form of a disk and the later
spoked wheel appeared in the Middle East, Asia and Egypt
as sun symbols, adding to the motif's impact.

216 SWASTIKA

Hitler distorted the meaning of an ancient symbol when he
made the swastika a feared emblem of Nazi Party power.
This wheel-like motif was originally benign. An image of
light trailing from each arm of a whirling cross, it suggested
the four directions of space and the creative power of the
sun. As such, it signified divine energy, from India across
the Middle East to Europe, as far north as Scandinavia. It
appears on the footprint and breast of the Buddha as an
emblem of cyclic regenerative power.

217 SPIRAL

Spiral symbols vary in meaning according to context, but can suggest the latent power of a spring – as in Maori facial tattoo patterns which mimic the phallic-like unfurling of ferns.

218 ZIGZAG

A traditional ideogram of the strike power of lightning, the Nordic zigzag was picked up and used by the Nazi SS in the form of a double zigzag insignia.

219 URAEUS

In Egypt, the power to give or take life was symbolized by a pharaonic diadem called the *uraeus*. It shows a female cobra, hood raised to strike, personifying the sun god, Ra, whose earthly representative the pharaoh was.

220 ORB

Circular forms draw their symbolic power from the implication of totality, and the orb or globe has been an emblem of all-inclusive power and worldly dominion at least from the time of the Roman Empire. It is an attribute of many gods portrayed in art.

See also:

216 Divinity and Sanctity, p.313

221 TRIANGLE

The triangle is a powerful geometric form. It combines mass with a penetrative point, suggesting solar aspiration as well as masculine force. The symbol is often linked to deities that represent three aspects of divine power.

222 PYRAMID

Drawing on the solar symbolism of the triangle, the mass, stability and durability of the Egyptian pyramid attempted to relate the power of the sun to the power of the pharaoh whose tomb it was. Few man-made symbols have looked so impressive or lasted so long.

223 FOUR

In number symbolism, four has the strongest links with the idea of omnipotence. It was associated with the four directions of space and the power of wind gods once thought to rule each quarter of the cosmos. Four pillars were the basic support for early buildings, and the Egyptians envisaged the same number of pillars holding up the sky.

224 HEAD

The power symbolism of the head helps to explain why headhunters decapitated their enemies. Their heads were thought to contain their life-force, strength and authority. Heads of monarchs or political leaders depicted on pillars or impressed on coins have similar emblematic significance. The intention is to suggest their power, even after death.

225 ARM

The arms of gods, leaders and heroes are also used as power symbols – most strikingly in the many statues and paintings of multiple-armed Indian gods. Often, each arm embodies a specific power to influence events on earth, the whole making up an image of omnipotence.

226 HAND

The executive role of the hand in human life and in war made it a very early symbol of power. Human hands appear at the end of solar rays in Egyptian religious art of the 2nd millennium BCE. Elsewhere in iconography, the hand is often depicted alone as an image of the power to direct events, protect, harm or heal. Hence the "laying-on of hands", a ritual action thought to work miracles or confer spiritual authority or blessings. A more grisly symbol was the **Hand of Glory (227)**, the name given to the hand of a hanged criminal in

See also:

221 Femininity and Maternity, p.124; Duality and Union, p.285

224 Temperance and Humility, p.190

England in the days when it was superstitiously thought to have curative power. Hangmen used to take fees from credulous bystanders for allowing them to place the hand on their bodies. As the most significant digit in man's evolutionary success, the **thumb (228)** can itself symbolize power. In the Roman coliseum it was enough to signal life or death for a defeated gladiator.

229 CHAKRAS

In Tantric doctrine, wheels (*chakras*) along the spine direct the flow of vital energy – symbols of the power gained by harnessing inner consciousness.

230 WEAPONS

Weapons are obvious symbols of power and appear as such in heraldry with both aggressive and defensive meaning. This is true even of the **hammer (231)**, usually an emblem of brute force linked to gods of thunder, notably the Nordic Thor, but also found on gravestones as a protective motif. A specific image of earthly power is the **lance (232)**, because of its association with cavalry, often the deciding factor in battle, and with the prestige and power of the horse.

233–5 HORNED ANIMALS

Strong connections between horns, weapons and masculine potency made a number of animals leading symbols of power. The strength, energy and aggressiveness of the **bull (233)** led to it being depicted as the incarnation or companion of many gods, ranging from Zeus in Greece to Shiva in India. It also symbolized the power of thunder and earthquake gods, as did the **ram (234)**. In Egypt, its horns became a specific symbol of solar power, as in images of the god Amun with curling horns. Alexander the Great adopted the ram as an emblem of his own all-conquering power when he extended his empire to Egypt. The **buffalo (235)** was another power emblem, associated with the whirlwind by the North American Plain Indians.

236 HORSE

Except in Africa and America, the horse was closely linked with military success in the ancient world, and therefore with the rise of dominant empires. Its size and speed also linked it with the power of the elemental forces of nature. Statues of leaders and heroes on horseback exploit this symbolism, the rider mastering the animal which itself represents power.

See also:

236 Fertility, p.46; Lust, p.240; Death, p.300

237 LION

The lions of Trafalgar Square are among the best-known symbols of British imperial power. But the history of the lion as a power emblem goes back to its identification with sun gods in the civilizations of Egypt and the Middle East. Using the solar glory of its golden coat and sheer physical presence, Egyptian iconography often pairs the lion with the disk of the sun. A human-headed lion, the world-famous Great Sphinx of Giza, simultaneously celebrates the power of the sun and of the pharaoh Khafre. Another hybrid, the **Griffin (238)**, combined the body of a lion with the head and wings of an eagle in Middle-Eastern statues symbolizing dual dominion over sky and earth.

239 JAGUAR

In Central and South America, the jaguar symbolizes the power of life and death. Shamans wore jaguar skins to identify themselves with the forces of protection and destruction.

240 TIGER

The tiger largely replaces the lion as an emblem of power in India and Asia. In Indian art, it is the mount of several gods – notably Shiva's fierce wife, Durga. To "ride the tiger" is to play with a dangerous power.

AUTHORITY ────────────────────

241 AXE

Chiefly authority is the symbolism of elaborately carved and decorated axes carried by leaders and used in tribal ceremonials for centuries. The flash and thud of the falling axe suggested it as an attribute of powerful Nordic thunder and lightning gods, and celestial associations may lie behind its ceremonial use elsewhere, particularly in Africa and Oceania. A double-headed axe was a cultic object of the Minoan civilization. It also appears in African art, sometimes as a female motif, suggesting that its authority symbolism may have been transferred from a king to his female attendants. In North America, the **tomahawk (242)**, which was adapted from more club-like tools and weapons after the arrival of Europeans, came to have status significance for tribal chieftains. Its symbolism was enhanced and personalized with paint and feathers.

243 MACE

Other weapons, like the mace, became purely symbolic after their usefulness in battle had disappeared. This spiked club, frequently elaborated with precious metals and even jewels, was carried by bodyguards for ceremonial purposes in Turkey as well as in northern European countries. In

England, it eventually became an emblem of royal authority. Hence the importance of the mace made for the House of Commons in 1649, symbolizing the passage of authority from king to parliament. Ecclesiastical and mayoral maces also denote status and authority.

244 CROSIER

Whereas force lies behind the symbolism of the mace, the crosier used in Church ritual symbolizes the leadership not of a warrior but of a shepherd. Its form, a staff incorporating a crook, dates back to ancient Sumeria, where it was a royal emblem of authority, and Egypt, whose pharaoh carried a crook signifying his role as shepherd of his people.

245 FASCES

This punitive authority emblem originated in the Etruscan civilization of Italy as a bundle of rods enclosing an axe. It was carried before Roman magistrates as a symbol of their power to scourge or behead offenders, the protruding axe-head being removed in Rome itself to acknowledge that its citizens could appeal against a death sentence. Mussolini took the name Fascism directly from the fasces, and his dictatorship soon turned it into an emblem of the state's coercive authority over its citizens.

246 FAN

The papal flabellum is a ceremonial development of the use of large fans to denote authority. They may, in ancient times, have been associated with fire rituals or linked with the power of the wind itself. The fan also had protective uses against flies and heat, and this may have helped to make it a status symbol both in Africa and Asia. Another authority symbol still carried by leaders of some African countries is the **fly whisk (247)**, which was also used ceremonially in

India and China. There may have been a symbolic connection with the threshing **flail (248)**, a pharaonic status symbol used in Egypt, but with more punitive significance.

249 ROD

Unlike more ceremonial staffs of office, the simple rod had magical links with authority in the ancient world by its association with the supposed powers of particular trees it was cut from, and by analogies with the snake and the phallus. As demonstrated in countless legends and folk stories, the rod carried by a charismatic individual took on an emblematic power itself, sometimes performing miracles. According to the Book of Numbers, the biblical Aaron, brother of Moses, gained the right to be chief priest of the Israelites when his rod flowered and produced almonds.

250 KEY

Keys were used as symbols of authority in many early civilizations and still are in some ceremonies of civic office. Newly consecrated popes receive diagonally-crossed keys of gold and silver as an emblem of supreme authority – in spiritual symbolism, the "keys of the kingdom".

251 RUDDER

The rudder or steering oar used in early shipping functioned as a decorative motif symbolizing authority in some sea-faring countries, and suggested the right to guide the affairs of a city or people. With providential symbolism, it became the attribute of several allegorical figures in Renaissance art.

252 CHARIOT

For sculptors and painters, the chariot made a splendid emblem of authority and rulership, conveying the idea of governance in dynamic images. The triumphal and solar symbolism that attached itself to the chariot from its earliest appearance as a machine of war later transferred itself to the spiritual plane, as can be seen by the Book of Kings, in which the prophet Elijah is transported to heaven in a chari-

See also:

252 Ascension and Axial Interchange, p.356

253 Health, p.82; Purity and Incorruptibility, p.220

255 Anger and Cruelty, p.248

ot of fire. The spiritual authority of divinities and religious figures is emphasized by the chariots they travel in, which are frequently drawn by creatures with specific symbolism.

253 JADE

Objects conferring authority often drew their symbolism from the precious materials from which they were made. An example is jade, the stone used in the seal of Chinese emperors, emblem of a celestial mandate. A jade of green nephrite called *pounamu* by the New Zealand Maori was used to make the sacred *mere*, a war club symbolizing chiefly authority.

254 CHAINS

Chains of office, worn by dignitaries as authority emblems, draw on the symbolism of community linkage to achieve common goals – they represent an authority that is usually temporary and dependent on cooperative leadership.

255 GIANTS

Giants in mythology, legend and folklore are thought by some psychologists to be symbols of an authority that is unwanted, onerous or tyrannical: in particular, parental authority – an emblematic meaning which ties in with their looming size.

SOVEREIGNTY

256 SUN

As the celestial body that outshone all others, the sun became an inevitable symbol of royalty. In the long Egyptian history of sun worship, pharaohs were so identified with the majesty of the sun itself that even priests of the great reforming pharaoh Akhenaten described him as being formed from solar rays. The symbolic links between royalty and the sun were transferred to the metal and hue **gold (257)**. At their accession, rulers of the Inca empire in Peru were once covered in resin sprayed with gold dust, hence Amazonian legends of El Dorado (the gilded one). At their death they were embalmed as "children of the sun" and seated in temples on golden thrones. Sixteenth-century English courtiers made play with the idea of Henry VIII as the sun around which they revolved, and in the following century the architecture and statuary of Versailles were designed to symbolize the absolute monarchy of Louis XIV as the Sun King.

258 PURPLE

The symbolism of purple as the colour of dignity and royalty derived from the high cost of producing purple dye in the ancient world. Tyrian purple, made from shellfish, was one of the earliest as well as the most expensive of durable cloth dyes. The British phrase "born in the purple" refers to the purple drapes hung in the room in which the children of Byzantine emperors were born.

259 PEACOCK·

The magnificent tail display of the male peacock gave this bird royal as well as solar symbolism, especially in Persia, where rulers sat on the jewelled "Peacock Throne" looted in the 18th century from the Mogul shahs of Delhi. In China, the bird was an emblem of the Ming Dynasty (1368–1644).

260 FLEUR-DE-LIS

The fleur-de-lis, a highly stylized lily looking more like a bearded iris, became the emblem of the French royal house in the 12th century; the flag initially carried it as an overall motif but later depicted three fleur-de-lis only, in celebration of the Holy Trinity. Its choice may have been influenced by associations between royalty and the lily in the Byzantine Empire. But legend also said that the Frankish chieftain Clovis had accepted the lily

See also:

259 Vigilance and Guardianship, p.140; Gluttony, Sloth, Avarice and Pride, p.193; Immortality and Eternity, p.329

as an emblem of purity on his baptism when he made himself king of France at the beginning of the 6th century.

261 THRONE

The ceremonial seats of sovereigns became powerful symbols of their status and rulership, raised up as they usually were on a dais. Precious materials and jewels have been used to heighten their associations with glory since the time of Solomon, who sat on a throne of ivory surmounting six steps. Thrones are sometimes shielded by a **canopy (262)**, symbolizing the approval and protection of still higher heavenly powers. In Hindu ritual, square canopies were used by priests, round ones by kings.

263 CROWN

Crowning has been used throughout history to confer legitimacy on a ruler, making the crown itself the supreme emblem of sovereignty. It draws on the protective symbolism of circularity and the power symbolism of the head.

A **golden wreath (264)** may have been the origin of the crown, whose appearance suggests the sun's aureole. This could have been adapted from simpler wreaths worn by heroes and athletic victors. In the Hellenistic period, some rulers wore the **diadem (265)**, a band carrying a central jewel, others decorated helmets. The fully developed crowns of medieval times often had hoops, associated with imperial power, together with royal decorative motifs such as lilies and increasingly lavish displays of gemstones.

266 SCEPTRE

Royal sceptres, like other staffs of office, are emblems of authority but have often been associated also with dominion over other regions and rulers – the symbolic meaning of the Roman ivory sceptre topped by an eagle. The sceptre of British monarchs is surmounted by an orb and cross, giving a spiritual dimension to the idea of global dominion. The monarch also carried a separate **orb (267)** topped by a cross – once the emblem of Holy Roman Emperors. In art, globes or orbs are held by many divinities or allegorical figures to imply universality, totality or omnipotence.

268 BEE

In Egypt, legend said that bees first fell to earth as the tears of the sun god Ra. Either because the pharaohs were themselves associated with the sun, or because the organization of the beehive suggested a monarchical system, the bee acquired royal symbolism not only in Egypt but in Greece and the Middle East. Following his Egyptian campaign, Napoleon Bonaparte had the bee motif worked into the design of his coronation robes as Emperor of France.

269 ROYAL BEASTS AND BIRDS

Symbolists have from early times picked out iconic animals and birds as emblematic images of the qualities possessed or desired by human rulers. As the "king of beasts" in Western tradition, the **lion (270)** has inevitable royal symbolism. Richard *Coeur-de-Lion* (lionheart) is one of many monarchs to have identified himself with its power, courage and solar symbolism. The royal lion hunt was a great theme of monumental art in western Asia. The lion was blended in statuary with the heads of Egyptian pharaohs. It is a royal emblem of England and Scotland, and, more recently, Haile Selassie, Emperor of Ethiopia, called himself "the lion of Judah".

See also:

268 Rebirth and Resurrection, p.338

The **elephant (271)** was also a symbol of royalty in Africa, and especially in India, where it appears in iconography as the mount of kings and divinities. In South America, the **jaguar (272)** is the iconographical royal animal corresponding to the lion. Both the **eagle (273),** in Rome and elsewhere, and the **falcon (274),** in Egypt and Peru, were symbolic lords of the air, linked with the souls of kings or emperors.

STRENGTH AND STABILITY

275 HERAKLES

Herakles is the most famous embodiment of physical strength in Western art, partly because Greek myth-making genius created a gripping saga of the "12 labours" he performed to make up for having killed his own children while deranged. He is a part-human, part-supernatural figure, drawn from more ancient myths of the Middle East, and strong enough to relieve for a time the Titan **Atlas (276)** in his task of holding the world aloft. Fantastic feats such as tearing mountains apart to form the Pillars of Herakles at the entrance to the Mediterranean were less popular with artists than almost-believable ones, such as forcing open the jaws of the Nemean lion and strangling it. As a reference to this story, Herakles often wears a lion skin in paintings, but most sculptors preferred to depict his musculature naked.

277 TOTEMS

Certain animals and plants were chosen in tribal societies throughout the world as totems which marked out the kinship of one clan or tribe from another, acquiring symbolic and sometimes sacred status. In North America particularly, many totemic creatures embodied qualities of strength and determination admired by the clan. Not all of them were fearsome. For example, the **salmon (278)** appears among tribes of the north Pacific coast as an emblem of strength for its heroic upriver battles to reach its spawning grounds.

279 BEAR

Outstanding among the larger totemic animals of North America was the bear, possibly because the almost human look of a standing bear increased the idea of kinship with its superhuman strength. Hence the folktales of bears mating with women and producing offspring. The bear was an ancestral figure not only to the Algonquin people but also to the Ainu of northern Japan. In Scandinavia, where the Berserkers wore bearskins into battle, it incarnated the might of the god Odin. Its strength could also symbolize protection, as in its association with the Celtic goddess Artio, protectress of Berne (city of the bear).

280 BOAR

In northern Europe and the Celtic world, the boar was a symbol of strength and resolution even more prominent than the bear. The boar helmets of Swedish warriors had both aggressive and protective significance, symbolism that may account for the many votive statues of boars discovered by archaeologists throughout Europe, where the boar was the attribute of many gods of war.

281 HIPPOPOTAMUS

The hippopotamus symbolizes brute animal strength in the Book of Job, where it appears under the name of Behemoth, a land creature corresponding to the **Leviathan (282)** of the deeps. Both appear as awesome symbols of forces that illustrate the puny strength of humankind and its need for divine help. In reverse symbolism, the Egyptian hippopotamus goddess Tawaret is depicted as an emblem of protective strength.

283–5 SUPPORTIVE ANIMALS

Many animals were, like the female hippo, symbols of supportive or defensive power. The **elephant (283)** is the prime example, appearing in both China and India as an emblem of moral strength, as is shown by its identification with the Hindu god of wisdom, Ganesha. Although it is also the mount of the thunder god Indra, its symbolic associations in Hindu tradition and art are usually of a quiet, peaceful kind. Ancient Hindu legends said the world was supported by a supernatural elephant standing on the legs of a **tortoise (284)**. This notion may have come from Chinese legends in which the cosmic tortoise Ao held the world up. Stone tortoises with this symbolism support the pillars of Chinese imperial graves. In Japan, the "world mountain" is carried by a tortoise. The **ox (285)** is another emblem of patient strength, a universally benevolent symbol.

286 PILLAR

The self-evidently supportive role of pillars made them symbols of strength and stability. In the architecture of the ancient world they were often built as free-standing objects with this meaning or embellished with the figures or heads of powerful gods. Two giant pillars flanked the porch of Solomon's temple as emblems of strength in duality. Strength is also the symbolism of the pillars that feature in such stories as that of the Irish hero Cuchúlainn strapping himself to

See also:

283 Chastity and Virginity, p.201

284 Longevity, p.41

a pillar to die on his feet, or of Samson crushing himself by pulling down the pillars of the Philistine temple.

287 LONG HAIR

Samson, whose strength ebbed as Delilah treacherously cut his hair, belonged to a Nazarite sect for whom long hair was a symbol not only of holiness but of strength. It remains so today for the Khalsa sect of Sikhs. Among many other communities, hair growth has been seen from the earliest times as an important symbol of the life-force.

288 BOW

Many strong men, heroes and gods are depicted in art holding a bow, which can symbolize strength. The classical example of its use in mythology is Homer's account of the great bow that only Odysseus can string and draw when he returns to Ithaca to claim his wife. In Japan, the bow is a samurai emblem of controlled physical, mental and spiritual power.

289 RED

In visual psychology, red is an advancing hue that looks heavier than others. This, together with its associations with fire, vitality and energy, has made it symbolically the strongest colour. It was linked with the power and strength of Mars and other war gods.

See also:

287 Love, p.230; Peace and Freedom, p.271

289 Love, p.231; Fame and Fortune, p.75

MASCULINITY AND VIRILITY

290   FATHER

A plethora of supreme sun, fire and war gods, represented
as mature or venerable males, reflects the symbolism of the
father as a dominating figure in the mainly patriarchal societies of the ancient world. This symbolism is particularly
marked in the areas of law-giving and punishment, and
mythology is full of legends in which the authority exercised
by the father is resented and overthrown by the son. The loving and giving God represented through the words of Jesus
in the New Testament marked a notable shift away from the
symbolism of the supreme father as a harsh autocrat.

291   MAN

Apart from emblematic male links with the sun and fire,
the masculine principle was represented in early symbolism
mainly by phallic objects such as upright stones, used as a
focus for rituals, and by penetrative objects. The naked male
figure could also symbolize humankind as a microcosm of the
universe, as in Leonardo da Vinci's drawing of a man with
arms and legs spread to suggest the four directions of space.

292   PHALLUS

The phallus itself can symbolize
creation, the life-force and the fertility

See also:

292 Protection, p.27

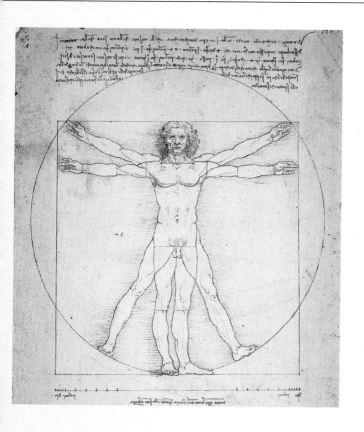

of nature or humans. Phallic amulets and talismans were used as charms against sterility and by farmers or fishermen to protect against crop failure or meagre catches of fish. Phallic funerary objects have also been found, probably signifying rebirth.

In the cave of Elephanta at Bombay, the **lingam (293)**, a massive cone of polished black rock representing the procreative power of Shiva, was the centre of worship involving ritual circumambulation – suggesting that it symbolized a world focus of spiritual forces as well as being a male fertility emblem.

294   **WEAPONS**

Weapons often have masculine and phallic significance, and appear in art with double meanings. Botticelli's famous painting *Mars and Venus* (1485) is an allegory of love's triumph over war and aggressive male desire, and depicts cupids, who are attending the love goddess, playing with the **lance (295)** of Mars while he lies sleeping (see pp.272–3).

In Phoenician iconography the **spear (296)** is the attribute of Hadad, their storm god, who thrusts a jagged spear into the earth in a double symbol of lightning and male fertilizing potency. With similar emblematic meaning, the Japanese creator god Izanagi uses a jewelled spear to stir the

primeval ocean. As he withdraws it, falling drops
form the first islands.

297 TORCH

The form and fire symbolism of the torch
or burning brand make it a male symbol
of both potency and desire, as the phrase
"carrying a torch" for someone still implies.
In wedding rituals, flaming torches had
this fertility significance.

298 OBELISK

Sacred obelisks constructed near Egyptian
temples, many of them now removed to
stand as monuments in other lands, appear
to have both phallic and solar meaning.
Their height and the fact that their pyra-
midical tips were sometimes covered
with gold show that they were primarily
designed to reflect the light of the sun
as part of solar worship. But their form
suggests the fertility symbolism of the
sun's rays penetrating the earth. The Celtic
maypole (299) also combines phallic and

fertility symbolism but its solar associations refer directly to the returning strength of the sun in spring. Its rituals developed from Greek and Roman festivals that were centred on the Classical resurrection god Attis. Sexual symbolism is extended by the pole penetrating a female disc or ring around which dancers revolve.

300 TORC

The attainment of manhood was linked in many early cultures with the right to become a warrior, a status often marked by emblems or body ornaments such as the Celtic torc. Worn round the neck, this metal ring with an opening at the front became a powerful symbol of male power and was often buried with the slain. Gauls of the 3rd century BCE fought naked but for the torc, as shown in the famous statue *The Dying Gaul*, carved by an unknown Roman in c.230 BCE.

301 BEARD

The beard was an important symbol of masculinity in some cultures, linked especially with male authority, which accounts for the frequent depiction

of bearded gods and rulers in Western art. In Egypt, young
or female rulers were sometimes shown with false beards.

302 KING

In ancient symbolism, the king is the archetype of male
perfectibility as well as a divinely sanctioned leader of his
people, and is often believed to have supernatural powers.
His virility and, in particular, his ability to father sons, was
bound up with his country's fortunes. There are many myths

in which the waning powers of a king (called the Fisher King in legends of the Holy Grail) are reflected in the decline of his realm.

303 ANIMALS

Male and female animals often differ sharply in symbolism. This is particularly true in Christian symbolism, where animal virility, admired in pagan cultures, gives rise to a negative symbolism of lewdness. The male **goat (304)** appears in both Hebrew and Christian traditions as an emblem of impurity or inappropriate sexual behaviour – a lasting tag confirmed by the disparaging term "he's an old goat". Yet the goat is a positive masculine emblem in India and in ancient Sumerian and Greek mythology.

The male ardour of the **bull (305)** is also celebrated by its association with many divinities who were often incarnated in bull form, specifically Zeus, who disguises himself as a bull to carry off Europa. Cretan bull worship led to the story that the Minoan queen Pasiphae fell madly in love with a white bull, later giving birth to the bull-headed Minotaur. Other animals with strong virility symbolism are the **stag (306)** and the **ram (307)**, both of whom were used in many cultures as positive emblems of the male principle. The **rhinoceros (308)** was another, so impressing Indian observers that the male magic of its powdered horn was widely sold to improve virility.

See also:

304 Fecundity and Plenty p.60

305 Purification, Atonement and Propitiation p.363

FEMININITY AND MATERNITY

309 WOMAN

Women appear early in the symbolic record as highly intuitive but also inconstant. Hence, perhaps, their role in legend and mythology as practitioners of magic, particularly the art of divination, and as guardians of oracles apt to deliver prophecies that could be read in more than one way. Ambivalence was carried through into Christian symbolism where personifications of vices or virtues were usually depicted as female. But most ancient emblems associated with women are protective and receptive, reflecting their importance as the carriers, givers and nourishers of human life. A long list of **receptacle forms (310)** have female symbolism, including boats, bowls, baskets, boxes, cups, cup-shaped flowers, goblets, pitchers, vases and wells, as is evident in both iconography and legend. On a vaster scale, the **sea (311)** itself is a feminine and maternal symbol.

312 MOTHER

The Mother Goddess has been a powerful figure throughout the world for many centuries. Early mythologies record the importance of the **Great Mother (313)** as a symbol not only of the Earth but of the source of divine, human and natural life. In the Greek system of Hesiod, she was Ge or Gaia, oldest of all divinities. Her counterpart in Asia Minor was Cybele, whose cult eventually reached Rome. A host of minor nature goddesses were worshipped as symbols of crop fertility. A less benign creative/destructive symbolism appears in the mythology and iconography of the **Dark Mother (314)**, personified by the Hindu goddess Kali and by other maternal figures with fearful aspects. Some personifications suggest the negative side of maternal love such as devouring possessiveness.

315 MOON

With some notable exceptions (Sumeria, Japan, Oceania and Teutonic cultures), lunar deities were feminine. The similar length of lunar and menstrual cycles created a powerful symbolic linkage, evident even in iconography of the Virgin Mary, who is sometimes shown with a crescent moon. This refers to a passage in the Book of Revelation (12.1), where a heavenly woman with the moon at her feet gives birth to a saviour. This image may have drawn on older traditions of virgin moon goddesses, such as the classical Artemis (Diana). Hunting societies owed much to the moon as the only source of light at night. The moon and womankind are often symbolically associated with occult practices, witchery, emotion and mutability.

See also:

315 Instinct, Intuition and the Unconscious, p.263; Immortality and Eternity, p.326

The human equivalent of the moon is the **Queen (316)**, emblematically the archetype of womanly perfection; her symbolic colour is silver.

See also:

317 Power p.90;
Divinity and
Sanctity, p.311

317 TRIANGLE

The triangle is a feminine symbol in China. This is only true elsewhere if it is inverted as an image of the female pubis, sometimes with a short extra line running to the bottom point. Synthesis is represented by intersecting triangles, sexual union by triangles with points touching.

318 VULVA

In Indian art, a stylized ring enclosing the base of stone phallic objects symbolizes female generative power. This dual imagery can also be found in pre-Columbian American art where the female genital symbol was a **lozenge (319)**, sometimes combined with a phallic snake. Lozenge motifs with fertility symbolism also decorated women's clothing in Central America. In Mali, a half lozenge with a point at the curved end signifies a young woman. The vulva and womb, or **yoni (320)**, are spiritualized in Tantric Buddhism where curved arcs represent gateways to the continuous rebirthing that leads to enlightenment. Among natural objects, the

shell (321) is a feminine symbol with erotic and fertility meaning, both through its hinged, containing form and its associations with the sea as the source of life. Shells such as the cowrie, with its smooth, labial curves, were used as fertility charms. In art, the shell can be a symbol of love and the vulva, as in Botticelli's beautiful painting of Venus (below).

322 MATERNAL ANIMALS

Most of the female animals who appear in mythology, art and folklore have positive symbolism through their associations with fecundity. The gentleness and passivity of the **cow (323)** are personified by many mother goddesses of both sky and earth. The Egyptian goddess of love and joy, Hathor, is shown with her horns cradling the sun. Vedic myths established the basis for the cow's sacred status in India, where milk, butter, cow manure and working cattle have underpinned the country's rural economy for centuries. Placed under the protection of Krishna, the cow was regarded as humankind's greatest gift from the gods. In effect, it embodies the nourishing self-sacrifice admired in women.

Legends of the **female goat (324)** and **bear (325)** are more linked to the nursing of babies. Fiercer protective symbolism appears in the **she wolf (326)**, said to suckle heroes, among them Romulus and Remus, the founders of Rome. Such stories help to explain why wolf ancestry was claimed for later leaders such as Genghis Khan.

327 CAT

Cats are identified as female rather than male symbols nearly everywhere, possibly because their night hunting associated

them with the moon.
Certainly, they appear as
lunar and female in Egypt,
where cultic worship of
the cat was widespread.
Originally, this was cen-
tred on the lioness god-
dess Sekmet, later merg-
ing into worship of the
fertility goddess Bastet,
depicted with the head
of a domestic cat.
Protective Egyptian
iconography shows a cat
as the ferocious killer of a
serpent which threatened
the sun on its nightly journey through the under-
world. In medieval

Europe, the cat's grace and suddenly unsheathed claws suggested feminine malice and disconcerting powers
of transformation. This negative symbolism also
appears in Japanese folklore of malign cats taking
over the bodies of women.

See also:

327 Evil, p.159

328 FEMALE HYBRIDS

Sinister animal hybrids with the heads of women haunt classical mythology, some personifying male fears of female vengeance. The foul, shrieking **Harpies (329)** and the implacable **Furies (330)** are cruel, punitive symbols. More often, female hybrids symbolize the allure of the feminine temptress and the risks of entrapment. Homer suggestively described Odysseus lashing himself to his ship's mast to resist the seductive song of the **Sirens (331)** while his men

rowed wearing earplugs. The most alarming of the Sirens were **Scylla and Charybdis (332)** who inhabited rocks in the Straits of Messina. Beneath their embodiment of such marine perils as whirlpools and reefs lies a darker sexual symbolism of suction and cannibalism. Although Greek art depicts the Sirens as birds with women's heads, by medieval times they had evolved into aquatic maidens like the mournful but dangerous **Lorelei (333)** of Rhine legend. **Mermaids (334)**, whose form may have been suggested by the whale-like nursing dugong of East African waters, have kinder, more wishful feminine symbolism for lonely sailors.

335 DOVE

The beauty of the dove and the softness of its cooing voice have for centuries made this bird an emblem of the tender wife. Its associations with loyalty and amiability may have been based partly on the idea that it mated for life. Its links with fertility, love and happiness are very old. The dove was sacred to the love godesses Aphrodite (Venus) and Astarte.

See also:

335 Chastity and Virginity, p.202; Peace, p.266

BEAUTY AND GRACE

336 BEAUTY AND GRACE PERSONIFIED

Beauty has mainly been represented by female emblems.
The divine archetype of female beauty is **Aphrodite (337)**,
better known in Western art by her Roman name, Venus.
She was the goddess of beauty as well as of love, concepts
indissolubly linked for the first time in history by the genius
of Greek sculptors who idealized the human form.

Grace is personified by Aphrodite's attendants the **Three Graces (338)**, a trio of naked or thinly veiled maidens (two facing forward, the centre one backward), a favourite subject for Renaissance artists, most famously Raphael. In the myth known as the Judgement of Paris, Aphrodite is also linked with **Helen of Troy (339)**, whose legendary beauty caused the Trojan War after the goddess helped Paris to abduct her. Helen symbolizes not just human beauty, but also its dangerous habit of sowing envy, rivalry and conflict.

340 SWAN

Beauty and grace combine in the symbolism of the swan, central to a myth in which Zeus chooses swan form to ravish Leda, the mother of Helen of Troy. The many tales in which swans transform themselves into lovely  women, and vice-versa, gave Tchaikovsky the theme of his ballet music for *Swan Lake*. The swan is also an emblem of the beauty and purity of light, both solar and lunar.

341 FULL MOON

The full moon has been an emblem of serene beauty for centuries, not least because it constantly renews itself and to this extent never fades as mortal beauty does. It is a Buddhist symbol of perfection.

342 FLOWERS

Whereas the moon represents an eternal beauty, flowers are the symbols of its poignant brevity. Chief among them in Western tradition is the **rose (343)**, used in countless poems as a metaphor for the beauty of the beloved. Roses were strewn throughout Aphrodite's temples. But the symbol of voluptuous beauty is the red rose celebrated by Robert Burns: "O, my Luve's like a red, red rose/That's newly sprung in June". Its equivalent in Egypt, India, Japan and China is the **lotus (344)**, its radiating petals a symbol of perfection. The **orchid (345)** is an emblem of refined beauty in China, whereas the more showy beauty of the **peony (346)** led to its adoption as an imperial flower. Another admired flower in China is the **camellia (347)** which symbolizes the beauty conferred by health.

348 CAT

Among animals, the cat is the leading emblem of beauty and grace. This is given a spiritual dimension in India where it symbolizes the state of beatitude. The cat's association with witchery may come partly from the close symbolic link between beauty and bewitchment. In many folk tales, witches appear as beautiful young women, some with cat-like powers of transformation.

349 BIRDS

Many birds are used as metaphors for graceful beauty, most obviously the swan (see p.131). Two have more ancient symbolism: the **partridge (350)** was associated in Greece with Aphrodite, in India with the seductive power of eyes and in China with elegance; the male **pheasant (351)** – in particular the golden pheasant, whose shining plumage was linked with the sun – is also an emblem of beauty in China. The pheasant and its relative, the even more ornamental **peacock (352)**, are the probable origin of legends about the miraculous phoenix.

353 PEARL

In gem lore, the pearl is the best-known emblem of feminine beauty, possibly because it has lunar symbolism and is associated with the sea-born goddess Aphrodite, often depicted in art emerging from a shell (see p.125). Another suggestion is that, like a woman, the pearl becomes more beautiful as it grows.

See also:

342 Mortality and Transience, p.36; Fertility, p.53

349 Knowledge and Learning, p.135

353 Fertility, p.55; Bad Luck, p.79; Health, p.83; Chastity and Virginity, p.202

KNOWLEDGE AND LEARNING

354 LIGHT

Light represents not only knowledge and intellect but also spiritual illumination. In ancient symbolism, its extensive use as a metaphor for divinity was associated with the direct light of the sun, appointed, according to Genesis, to rule the day. A distinction was made between this and the reflected light of the moon, which became linked with thought and rational knowledge. But in both cases the basis for the symbolism is simple: light enables us to explore and know the world around us, darkness leaves us in blind ignorance.

355 BLUE

The celestial symbolism of blue made it a Chinese emblem of scholarship and gave it a wider meaning of spiritual knowledge in Buddhism. For the same reason, blue is still generally thought of as the least material shade of the spectrum, suggesting the calm life of the conscious mind, as it does in Jungian psychology.

356 MERCURY (HERMES)

In planetary symbolism and in Renaissance art Mercury, messenger of the gods, personifies reason, swiftness of thought, knowledge

See also:

354 Goodness and Benevolent Power, p.144; Divinity and Sanctity, p.304

355 Grief, Mourning and Melancholia, p.255

and eloquence. Some paintings show him as a teacher, especially of Cupid. Under his Greek name, Hermes, the god appears in Greek mythology as more cunning than learned. But he later became associated with the Egyptian god of writing, Thoth, giving the name "hermetic" to a body of ancient learning, much of it occult.

357 BIRDS

The link between communication and finding things out which made Mercury a personification of reason also applies to birds, whose flight between sky and earth gave them ancient associations with higher realms of knowledge. They often appear in folktales as sources of information.

Thoth, the Egyptian patron deity of scribes, sometimes appears with the head of an **ibis (358)**. This wading bird became a sacred emblem of secret knowledge, sometimes mummified and buried in royal tombs as a guide to the underworld. More famous as a symbol of erudition is the **owl (359)**. It was credited by the Greeks with foresight, probably because of its ability to see and hunt at night using its exceptionally large eyes. With this meaning, it became the attribute of the Athenian goddess of learning, Athene. Coins struck in her honour had an owl on one side. An owl perching on a pile of books later

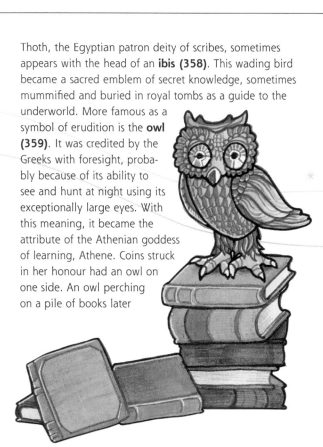

became a popular motif, leading to the idea of the "owlish" book-loving scholar.

360   BOOK

In art the book is, for obvious reasons, the most common emblem of learning, accompanying allegorical figures personifying history, philosophy and literature. It also appears as a symbol of the Word of God in paintings of saints, prophets and apostles, including John the Evangelist, who is shown swallowing the Book of Revelation.

361   ELEPHANT

The elephant's sagacity and longevity made it an important emblem of intelligence in India, associations also found among some African peoples. The elephant-headed god Ganesha represents worldly wisdom in the Indian pantheon and is patron of the book trade.

See also:

359 Evil, p.160
361 Goodness and Benevolent Power, p.149; Happiness and Joy, p.251

VIGILANCE AND GUARDIANSHIP

362 **VIGILANCE PERSONIFIED**

Vigilance was a preoccupation of late medieval society in Europe, and a quality expected of leaders in an age of constant warfare. It was personified in art by a young woman accompanied by a **crane (363)** holding up a stone in one claw. Bestiaries of the day had taken this symbolism from a legend mentioned by Aristotle in which the crane was said to use a stone to keep itself awake while waiting for prey – if it fell asleep, the splash of the dropped stone would wake it.

364 **DRAGON**

The dragon sometimes personifies vigilance in art, a symbolism drawn from the many legends and myths in which it is the keen-eyed guardian of treasures such as the golden apples of the Hesperides and the Golden Fleece. Its name comes from the Greek *drakonates* (large snake), a word which itself derives from a verb meaning "to see sharply".

365 **COCK**

The cock's alertness, particularly to dawn light, made it one of the best-known emblems of vigilance. Hence its traditional use on church weather-vanes, where the symbolism is shifted

See also:

364 Evil, p.156

365 Charity, Care and Compassion, p.173; Fortitude and Courage, p.184

to the religious plane,
the cock standing watch-
ful guard against evil
and calling backsliders
to church. A link between
vigilance and foreknowledge
is the probable reason for
the use of roosters in occult rites
of divination among some tribal
cultures in Africa.

366 GOOSE

Few domestic animals are quicker to spot strangers than
geese, as a group of geese sacred to Juno showed in 390 BCE
on the Capitoline hill in Rome. According to a celebrated
story, their cackling roused the garrison when Celtic warriors
tried to slip over the wall forming the last bastion of the
city's defences during a 6-month siege. Reading divine inter-
vention into this incident, Rome created a golden goose icon
to be carried in processions as a symbol of vigilance.

367 LYNX

In art, the lynx represents the sense of sight – not surprisingly
given its remarkable vision. For this reason, it also became

an emblem of an acute, spying watchfulness. Superstition said it could see through walls.

368 EYE

Eye motifs often appear alone as symbols of vigilance or omniscience. The most famous example is the Egyptian **wedjat (369)** or Eye of Horus, the falcon-headed sky god. This decorative emblem of a painted eye surrounded by curved and spiralling lines, based on hawk-like facial markings, symbolized the god's strict watch over religious laws and ceremonials. In the sense of vigilance against evil, it was used as a protective device on amulets. Eyes were also painted on some Egyptian tombs.

The eye-like markings on the tail of the male **peacock (370)** were taken in classical mythology as emblems of vigilance. According to legend, they were the multiple eyes of Argus Panoptes, the all-seeing guard used by Hera to keep watch over her rival Io. The same symbolism in a kindlier aspect appears in Tibet, where the peacock is the vigilant companion of Amitabha, the compassionate Buddha of Infinite Light.

See also:

370 Gluttony, Sloth, Avarice and Pride, p.193

371 Death, p.299

371 DOG

Dogs have ambivalent symbolism as protective guardians, often appearing as ferocious watchdogs like Cerberus, the three-headed snapping keeper of the gates to Hades. But in the Celtic world, and in Christian symbolism generally, their vigilance is benign. Black and white dogs were symbols of the evangelical Dominican order whose friars were "dogs of the Lord"

Virtues and Vices

Goodness and Benevolent Power . 144

Evil 152

Innocence 164

Truth and Deceit 166

Charity, Care and Compassion . . . 171

Faith and Hope 174

Justice 180

Fortitude and Courage 182

Temperance and Humility 187

Gluttony, Sloth,
Avarice and Pride 192

Chastity and Virginity 196

Prudence and Wisdom 205

Fidelity and Loyalty 212

Purity and Incorruptibility 216

GOODNESS AND
BENEVOLENT POWER

372   LIGHT

Centuries of sun and fire worship lay behind the choice of light as the ultimate symbol of the force of good in the world. This symbolism was made specific in the 6th-century BCE teachings of Zoroaster (Zarathustra), the Iranian religious reformer and probable author of the *Gathas*. He initiated, and his followers developed, the concept of a fundamental struggle between dominions of good and evil, one ruled by **Ahura Mazda (373)**, who had chosen the light, and the other by a supreme Lord of Darkness, Ahriman. This stark dualistic system influenced Judaism, Christianity and Islam and planted the explosive idea of the Devil as a motivator of human wrongdoing.

374   ANGELS

Since medieval times, angels have been the most popular personifications of goodness in Western art, acting as inter-mediaries between heaven and earth. Their name, taken from the Greek *angelos* (messenger), suggests their primary symbolic role as bearers of good news. But other functions were proposed for them, ranging from steering the stars – a Greek notion

See also:

374 Evil, p.153;
Gluttony, Sloth,
Avarice and
Pride, p.194

supported by Aristotle – to battling with evil. Winged guardian figures of the ancient Middle East may have provided models for later artists, who depicted angels first as male. Fra Angelico,

early in the 15th century, was influential in showing them as beautiful young women. Christian theology envisaged nine angelic orders. Nearest to God were **seraphs (375)**, usually painted red, and **cherubs (376)**, blue. Both were thought to have six wings. In Baroque art, cherubs were often shown as chubby, winged infants, striking a more playful note carried over into modern Christmas traditions in which angels symbolize joy as much as goodness.

Archangels (377) had individual and specific symbolism because they intervened in human affairs. The best-known are Gabriel, herald of the Annunciation, whose attribute is the lily of purity; Michael, guardian and instrument of justice, who carries a sword or scales; and Raphael, who holds a staff as protector of pilgrims, travellers and children.

378 CIRCLE

Circles seem always to have had beneficial, even spiritual symbolism, probably because the sun, moon and planets, which were then thought to guide human life, presented themselves as circular not only in their form but in their apparent cyclic movement around the earth. The 3rd-century Greek school of philosophy, now known as Neo-Platonist, took the circle as an ideogram of the One, the wholly good, towards which the human spirit should aspire. As a "perfect" geometric form without divisions and alike at all points, the circle suggests totality as well as eternal continuity, union as well as protective containment. In Christian symbolism, the Trinity was sometimes shown as three overlapping circles. At a much simpler level, the fairy ring of folk tradition has mystic protective and beneficial significance.

379 MIRROR

In both Christian and Islamic tradition, a bright mirror is an emblem of virtue, a dull one the opposite. The mirror's association with the principle of good goes back to ancient ideas about reflective surfaces that captured the divine light of the sun and moon. This positive symbolism led to the belief that mirrors could reject evil or drive it away, and to the idea that the Devil had no reflection. In Japan, a bronze mirror, Yatano Kagami, kept in the nation's most important Shinto shrine, represents the return to the world of the sun goddess, Amaterasu. In myth, she was tempted from her hiding place by a magical mirror, which led her to believe that the world could reflect her own goodness. In Shinto legend, a giant mirror that can detect evil-doers chooses those who enter Hell. In

See also:

379 Bad Luck, p.79

China, the mirror is one of the "Eight Precious Things of Buddhism". It symbolizes the enlightenment that comes from understanding the illusory nature of the world.

380 STONE

Stone is a common biblical metaphor for reliability and integrity. It was also sometimes used as a mystic symbol of hidden blessings, as in the story of water springing from the rock struck by the rod of Moses.

Beneficial divine power was also the symbolism of gemstones such as the **diamond (381)**, a crystallized mineral which in Indian tradition was said to form the throne of Buddha. **Jade (382)** had a similar elevated value in China. It was so strongly identified with virtue that it symbolized not only moral purity but also justice, truth, courage, harmony, loyalty and benevolence.

383 ASIAN DRAGON

In complete contrast to its Western symbolism, the dragon is a major emblem of benevolent power in Asia, particularly in China. As the motif of the Han dynasty, the five-clawed dragon Lung was a yang guardian emblem, its strength equated with the elemental forces of storm, thunder, lightning and hurricanes. It brought

See also:

383 Evil, p.156

the gifts of spiritual knowledge, happiness, fertility and immortality. Chinese dragon processions celebrate the germinating blessings of rain.

384 ELEPHANT

In India, the elephant has embodied a whole spectrum of virtues, possibly because the elephant-headed god, Ganesha,

was the patron deity of writing and therefore of administrators. Hence the symbolic association between the elephant and the qualities or aims of good government, especially wisdom, prudence, intelligence, peace and successful harvests.

385 COW

The cow is a universally benevolent and auspicious symbol. The reverence paid to it in India depended not only on its productivity but also on the fact that its patience, equanimity and harmlessness presented an image of goodness in harmony with quietist elements in Indian philosophy and religion, particularly Buddhism and Jainism.

386 BEE

Few, if any, creatures have symbolized more ethical virtues than the bee. Apart from being associated with many divinities, its industrious habits and social organization were a gift to the writers of homilies. The Christian monastic community was equated with a beehive. Bees were emblems of diligence, technical and administrative skill, unselfishness, sociability, cleanliness, chastity, creativity, sagacity, courage and spirituality. The 12th-century mystic Bernard of Clairvaux likened the bee to the Holy Ghost.

The virtues ascribed to the bee had much to do with the beneficial powers of its **honey (387)**. An important source of sugar in the ancient world, honey was thought to have medicinal value and was sometimes used for anointing and embalming. It thus came to have celestial symbolism and was said to be the food of gods, heroes, seers and poets. Its links with eloquence led to a legend that Pythagoras had been brought up on it as a baby.

388 GREEN

The generally benevolent symbolism of the colour green derives from its ancient associations with the renewal of plant life in spring. Like most colours, it also has negative meaning in some contexts, but it is the colour of divine providence in the Islamic world. Its symbolic associations with the health of both the planet and of humankind are evident in its emblematic use as the colour of pharmacy and of the ecology movement.

See also:
388 Envy and Jealousy, p.246

EVIL

389 DARKNESS

Primeval fears of the unknown, together with the early link between light and divinity, made it inevitable that darkness would become the emblematic opposite of goodness – evil. Despite examples of darkness having positive symbolic value, it more often stands for negative ideas and events – death, mourning, widowhood, melancholia, despair, madness, concealment, obscurity, ignorance, blindness, nothingness. The many modern English idioms that use **black (390)** to denote misfortune, rejection or disaster draw on a long tradition of European superstitions in which darkness and evil went hand in hand. One of the earliest known maleficent symbols is the **Black Sun (391)** of ancient Babylonian cosmology. In Tibetan Buddhist art, **black stones (392)** represent bad deeds that are weighed against white stones of good deeds in calculating a person's spiritual progress.

393 SATAN

See also:

393 Fame and Fortune, p.75

394 Goodness and Benevolent Power, p.144

Satan's role as Prince of Darkness, the most famous personification of evil, has a shorter history than usually supposed. Simple societies of the ancient world saw evil as chaos, disorder, illness and other misfortunes, rather than as moral wickedness. Catastrophes were the work not of a single, ruling devil but of capricious gods or malign demons who could be placated by gifts or sacrifices.

At first, in the Old Testament, Satan was merely a servant of Yahweh, sent to try or test men. The symbolism of this figure was evident in his name, which meant "adversary". Christian theology introduced a radical change by associating him with **Lucifer (394)**, a fallen angel whom God cast down to hell for the sin of pride, according to the prophet Isaiah. The Church decided that this had happened before the Creation and that thereafter Satan had dedicated himself to evil. The model for this more malevolent and powerful figure was **Ahriman (395)**, a dark creator spirit who chose evil in the dualistic light/dark theology of the Iranian magus Zoroaster. This idea also influenced Islam, where the spirit of evil was Shaitan or **Iblis (396)**.

397 DEVILS

Evil, temptation and general immorality were symbolized in medieval Western art not only by Satan himself (see pp.152–3) but also by lesser devils representing his followers. The characteristic figure that emerged was a hybrid with a distinct similarity to classical depictions of the pagan god **Pan (398)** and his followers, the **Satyrs (399)**. In a religious age bent on suppressing animal passions, this rough, shepherd deity with his seductive pipes and goatish features suggested bestiality. The devilish images that dominate art have forked tails, horns, cloven hoofs and sometimes bat wings. They carry pitchforks or spears to prod sinners to Hell. Smaller black figures representing demonic possession crawl from the mouths of exorcised victims. The **Mephistopheles (400)** of dramatic Faustian poems by Marlowe and Goethe is a more subtle satanic agent. His offer to satisfy Faust's wishes in return for his soul gave literary form to medieval superstitions that people who were too clever or successful must have made pacts with the Devil. In psychological terms, Mephistopheles symbolizes the temptations of self-gratification.

401 WITCH

For centuries before the birth of Christ, witches were eerie but respected practitioners of the art of prophecy. It was rising belief in the existence of a powerful Devil that persuaded the medieval world that witches were his dangerous servants. They became, effectively, a symbol not of the use of occult powers but of their misuse. In the witch-hunting hysteria that reached its height in Europe between the 15th and 17th centuries, thousands of harmless women were drowned or burned because they were thought to worship Satan at **witches' sabbaths (402)**. This idea was a symbolic inversion, suggesting that evil was abroad on God's emblematic day of rest. Traditional symbols of witchcraft include owls, black cats, toads, wolves, foxes, snakes, poisonous herbs and dreadful sacrificial offerings such as dead babies.

403 SNAKE

The snake has extraordinarily extensive and varied symbolism, but in Western sacred art it is primarily an emblem of evil. The Virgin Mary is shown trampling it underfoot, and so are other figures or creatures representing purity, faith and other virtues. The tradition of snakes being enemies of humankind goes back to the Book of Genesis in which a snake tempts Eve to eat forbidden

See also:
403 Health, p.80

fruit – an allegory of a sacrilegious attempt to acquire god-like powers. This story may have been a Hebrew warning against Mediterranean and Middle Eastern fertility cults, which used sacred snakes as phallic symbols. The Book of Revelation later referred to "that old serpent called the Devil". In paintings of the Crucifixion, a serpent at the foot of the cross or wound around it symbolizes the original sin that led to the Fall.

404   DRAGON

Like the snake, the dragon is a predominant symbol of evil in Western tradition, emerging from early mythologies as a reptilian embodiment of chaos, known in Sumeria from ancient times as "adversary". In pagan legends generally, it is usually a straightforward symbol of disaster, tyranny or cruelty. But it became, in Christian symbology, a bestial fire-breathing image of the Devil and his infernal realm. The beast appears several times in the Book of Revelation, once as a great red dragon with seven heads and ten horns. Paintings showing dragons in combat with saintly warriors, such as George or the Archangel Michael, are allegories of the conquest of evil. Less militant figures leading a dragon on a chain or cord represent faith tam-

See also:

404 Vigilance and Guardianship, p.138; Goodness and Benevolent Power, p.148

ing disbelief or virtue taming vice. The dragon shares some of Satan's physical characteristics – bat wings and horns – and is usually shown with powerful eagle legs, a scaly body and a barbed tail, which may have knots indicating its defeat. The sea serpent is a close relative, but more often appears in depictions of classical myths in which it is defeated by heroes such as Perseus.

405 HYDRA

Another dragon-like mon-ster of Greek myth-making, the Hydra was a many-headed water snake lurking in the swamps of Lerna, near Argos. Killing it was the second of the "12 labours" of Herakles. Each time he cut off one of his heads, two more grew, until he solved the problem by cauterizing the stumps with fire. The Hydra symbolizes the multiple nature of evil and the difficulty of permanently conquering vices that have become habitual.

406 BASILISK

Also known as the cockatrice, this hybrid creature of fable haunted medieval Europe as a specific symbol of the poison spread by the Devil – a throwback to much earlier beliefs in which evil and illness were closely interlinked. Based probably on Egyptian images of the cobra raised to strike, it was depicted with a cock's head and wings on a serpent's body and was sometimes shown wearing a crown. It had fiery, venomous breath and its gaze could kill. Hence the expression "basilisk-eyed". Unlike heroic myths of the dragon, the basilisk was an emblem of evil and disease working at the level of ordinary rural life.

407 CAT

The medieval idea that a black cat might be the Devil in disguise has echoes in Celtic folklore. Greek mythology may also have contributed to this negative symbolism as cats attended the underworld deity **Hecate (408)** in her capacity as goddess of witches, ghosts and necromancy. Shakespeare's reference to Hecate appearing to the witches in *Macbeth*, and his description of her as "the close contriver of all harms", associated her with occult evil.

See also:

407 Femininity and Maternity, p.126; Beauty and Grace, p.132

409 Health, p.81

The cat's satanic symbolism as a familiar of witches owed something to its powers of transformation, its ability to see in the dark and its fondness for night hunting. To the superstitious, its stealth, mood changes and ability to suddenly unsheath its claws or contract its pupils might have added to the general image of untrustworthiness. Most damningly, a cat was often the sole companion of the lonely old women who were easy targets for witch-hunters.

409 TOAD

The toad is a highly ambivalent symbol in medieval superstition, linked with evil, darkness, lust and avarice but also with legends in which toads carried a

jewel in their foreheads. Its toxic secretions could either cause harm or work miracles – which accounts for the belief that toads were used in the hellish broths contrived by witches, whose familiars they were thought to be.

410 OWL

The owl appears in art as the companion of Night personified. Its nocturnal, predatory flights, eerie cry and staring eyes linked it with the powers of darkness and with occult powers to see into the future. These sinister aspects of the bird led to it becoming a symbol of death in the Americas, India and ancient Egypt. Chinese superstitions said young owls pecked out their mother's eyes. In medieval Europe, despite the owl's well-known associations with wisdom, the demonic side of its symbolism made it another reputed familiar of witches.

411 BAT

The bat has for centuries been a victim of superstitions that it was an enemy of light, a symbolism made specific in South American images of a bat opening its mouth to swallow the sun. It was widely credited with occult powers of evil. Curiously, this meant that in Europe sick people sometimes had bats applied to their bodies in the belief that they would draw out

pestilence. A similar protective motive explains
the ancient practice of nailing bats to doors in
order to frighten demons. Christian symbolism
made a comparison between the bat's rejection of the light
and sinners rejecting the teachings of Jesus. Demons and
dragons wore bat wings, and bats were depicted fluttering
about the dwellings of witches. In Goya's depiction of his
own suffering, *The Sleep of Reason*, bats symbolize madness.

Early in the 19th century, a literary cult of the **vampire
(412)** promoted the false idea that bats could prey on the
blood of humans. This was suggested by the habits of a
small South American species which lapped the blood of
animals. Bat characteristics were soon added to the image
of "undead" corpses stalking the night. Tales of such nocturnal predators had long haunted Balkan and Greek folklore
and it needed only the imagination of the Victorian writer
Bram Stoker to bring together these superstitions in the
menacing figure of **Dracula (413).**

See also:

410 Prudence,
Wisdom, p.206

414   FOX

Like the cat, the fox was a slinking nocturnal predator – an
animal whose wiliness suggested to Christian symbolists the
guile of the Devil. The medieval Church made it an emblem
of evil, malice and, above all, of hypocritical duplicity.

However, this symbolism was turned against the Church itself in the vastly popular stories of **Reynard (415)**, the inventive fox which became almost a hero figure in Germany, Flanders and France (the famous *Roman de Renard* tales). In this literature, in spite of its destructiveness, the fox acts as a witty satirist of feudal society. A similar ambivalence can be seen in the figure of **Loki (416)**, with whom the fox is associated in Nordic, Teutonic and Celtic mythology. The mean tricks played by this god suggest him as a precursor of the Devil, but he is too jokey to symbolize pure evil.

417 WOLF

The wolf also has ambivalent symbolism, but in the forested areas of Europe it was predominantly a symbol of ferocious rapacity. Because Jesus was the Good Shepherd and his believers were his flock, the wolf preying on sheep fitted neatly into Christian symbolism as an image of the Devil and a personification of heresy.

In the "Ragnarok", the

Nordic myth of the end of the world, a giant wolf called
Fenris (418) swallows the sun, a devouring symbolism
which also appears in Celtic legends. In Germany and eastern
Europe, tales of **werewolves (419)** have been told for centuries. More frightening versions of the big, bad wolf of fairytales, these creatures were men in wolf form who were said
to feed on young children and corpses. Rapacious sexuality
was another component of their symbolism. They embodied
fears of demonic possession, which is also evident in tales of
witches transforming themselves into wolves.

420 **LEOPARD**

Although its courage resulted in its use as an English battle
emblem, the leopard was a symbol of sin in Christian tradition. This seems to have been based on a biblical analogy
between a leopard's inability to change its spots and the
difficulty of changing evil
habits. Shamans in Africa
and Asia used leopard
skins to show their com-
mand of the animal's
ferocious power. It was
associated in Egypt with
the violent god Seth.

INNOCENCE

421–3 LAMB AND CALF

Innocence is personified in Christian art by a young woman with a **lamb (421)**. The gentleness and meekness of the lamb made it the most poignant of all emblems of Christ's sacrifice. Jesus was the "paschal lamb", the "sacrifice without blemish", crucified for the sins of the world yet sinless himself. The **calf (422)** sometimes appears in iconography with the same meaning.

The symbolism of both animals substitutes for the **child (423)**, an obvious symbol of innocence, yet one seldom used with this specific meaning in art, except in paintings of "The Massacre of the Innocents" – the killing of male infants in Bethlehem at the order of Herod. In Victorian funerary symbolism, the lamb is the image most often carved on the gravestones of children.

> **See also:**
>
> **424** Grief, Mourning and Melancholia, p.255; Defeat, Cowardice and Betrayal, p.280

424 WHITE

As the symbolic opposite of black, white is a colour of innocence, as well as of the novice or neophyte. Hence the word "whitewash" to describe the covering up of guilt. The symbolism of sexual innocence lies behind the custom of wearing white at baptisms, confirmations and weddings. White flowers can have the same emblematic meaning, particularly the **lily (425)**, a universal symbol of purity. In Christian art, the flower is often associated with the Virgin – in Domenico Veneziano's *The Annunciation* (c.1445), for example, the angel Gabriel is shown kneeling before her with a lily in his hand.

426 NAKEDNESS

Nudity is a metaphor for primal innocence in the Book of Genesis. Adam and Eve are naked in the Garden of Eden until they eat from the forbidden tree of the knowledge of good and evil. They reveal their guilt by dressing themselves in fig leaves when they hear God approaching. Following this symbolism, early Christian ascetics and saints often went naked. For several sects, including the Adamites and Dukhobors, disrobing meant an emblematic return to the original state of innocence.

427 WASHING

Innocence is sometimes personified in paintings by a young woman washing her hands. Apart from its wider symbolism in rituals of purification or initiation, rinsing with water could represent absolution from guilt, as suggested by Pontius Pilate's action in washing his hands to indicate that he did not take responsibility for the crucifixion of Jesus.

TRUTH AND DECEIT

428 TRUTH PERSONIFIED

Truth is represented in Western art by the figure of a woman shown with the sun's rays or holding its glowing disk in her hand. The symbolism is that the sun reveals all. In a Bernini sculpture, she stands on a globe – truth rising above the petty deceptions of the world. In painting, she sometimes appears as the daughter of **Father Time (429)**, who lifts aside a veil from her body to illustrate the maxim that "truth will out" with the passage of the years. A laurel wreath implies that she will always defeat her enemies, slander and falsehood. She may also be seen reading from a book symbolizing truth.

430 DECEIT

Deceit is also shown in art as a young woman, but this time with the scaly body of a **snake (431)**. The snake's forked tongue was famously used as a metaphor for falseness among North American Indians. Another emblem of deceit is the **mask (432)**. In Western paintings and sculptures, this sometimes hides the face of an old crone behind the image of a beautiful girl. Animal symbols of deceit include the **fox (433)** and the **wolf (434)**.

435 MIRROR

Although the mirror often has other symbolism in art, it is an important emblem of truth, as demonstrated by the old saying, "the mirror never lies". In Japanese mythology, the children of the creator god Izanagi are instructed to kneel before a mirror and examine their deepest thoughts to rid themselves of self-deceit and evil desires. More dramatically, Shakespeare's Hamlet seizes his royal mother and shouts at her: "You may not go until I set you up a glass where you may see the inmost part of you".

436 HEART

The heart was often thought of as the repository of the soul or innermost spirit of a person, as is evident in Egyptian funerary customs – it was the only major organ that was not removed from the body during the process of mummification. The heart became a symbol of moral courage and, by association, truth. People still profess their sincerity by saying "hand on heart". Artists of the Renaissance represented this symbolism by means of a **peach (437)** with a leaf attached, the peach representing the heart and the leaf the tongue speaking its truth.

438 PRECIOUS STONES

The integrity and hardness of some gemstones associated them with truth, particularly when they were also symbols of the heart. This was true of **jade (439)** in China. The etymological link between adamant and **diamond (440)** explains how it became the most popular stone for engagement rings, its impregnability suggesting sincerity and therefore truth. Sapphire, onyx and lodestone also symbolize truth.

441 SWORD

In the sense that it cuts through falsehood, the sword is one of the emblems of justice that also doubles as an emblem of truth. The double-edged sword was a symbol of the tongue speaking the truth in the Book of Revelation, where it protrudes from Christ's mouth. Paintings of the archangel Michael show him with sword and **scales (442)**, which imply that the truth is often found only through a process of impartial weighing up. The Egyptian goddess of truth, Ma'at, is also depicted with scales.

443 LAMP

Truth is closely linked in symbolism with light – the sun, the moon (spiritual truth in the darkness of ignorance), the lightning flash (all-revealing clarity), and the light of lamp, lantern, torch or candle.

444–7 NINE AND CUBE

In mystical Hebrew tradition, **nine (444)** was the number of truth, a symbolism based on the idea that it was an incorruptible number. When it is multiplied by any other digit, the two digits produced add up to nine. The same association with consistency accounts for the **cube (445)** being a geometric symbol of truth. All six of its faces are exactly the same. Significantly, the cube is the Islamic centre of faith, the shape of the **Ka'aba (446)** which is the focus of pilgrimages to Mecca and is built as a double cube. It incorporates at its eastern corner the venerated "Black Stone". **Meteorites (447)**, fragments of which form the Black Stone, were themselves emblems of spiritual truth in the ancient world and are known to have been worshipped as messages from celestial gods.

CHARITY, CARE AND COMPASSION

448 **CHARITY PERSONIFIED**

The old meaning of charity is selfless love – for others and for God. For St Paul, this was the greatest of the three so-called Theological Virtues – faith, hope and charity. Four other essential virtues, known as the Natural or Cardinal Virtues had been proposed by Greek philosophy – prudence, temperance, fortitude and justice. Together, these seven virtues were taken as the basis of Christian morality.

Charity itself is usually personified in Western art by a woman suckling two infants, although in medieval art she appeared as a young woman clothing or feeding the poor. She often has a bundle of clothes or basket of food and holds a candle signifying divine benevolence, or a flaming **heart (449)** symbolizing compassion for others and love for God.

450 **GOOD SAMARITAN**

A more specific personification of charity is the Good Samaritan praised by Jesus in the famous parable recounted by the apostle Luke. Two Jewish travellers ignore an injured man who has been robbed by thieves and left by the side of the road. But a passing Samaritan tends the injured man's wounds with oil and wine, binds them and carries him to an inn to recuperate. This story, symbolizing what it means to be a good neighbour, had added significance because Samaritans were a separate sect of Israelites shunned by many Jews.

451 BIRDS

In Baroque art of the 17th century, birds sometimes appear with the figure of Charity as emblems of charitable love, notably the **pelican (452).** The sight of pelicans dipping their bills to feed their young led the writers of medieval bestiaries to suggest that they were tearing their breasts to provide a sustaining flow of blood. With the same meaning of self-sacrifice, the pelican is sometimes shown at the foot of the cross in crucifixion scenes, along with the **phoenix (453),** a legendary bird said to immolate itself.

The **hen (454)** with its chicks is used as an animal personification of charity; the **cock (455)** is also a symbol of loving care because it finds food and drops it for hens and chicks to eat before it feeds itself.

456 HAND OF FATIMA

The hand is an obvious symbol of charity, even when it is used pejoratively in the term "hand-outs". One of the most famous decorative emblems in the Islamic world is the Hand of Fatima. The five fingers on the hand of Muhammad's daughter proclaim that charity is one of the fundamental virtues, together with faith, prayer, pilgrimage and fasting.

457 BREASTS

The naked breast which symbolizes charity in religious paintings also once had emblematic meaning as an appeal for compassion and mercy. This is implied in paintings that show women of a defeated tribe kneeling before their enemies and displaying their breasts.

See also:

456 Protection, p.26; Power, p.91

FAITH AND HOPE

458   FAITH PERSONIFIED

Faith is often shown in sacred art as a helmeted woman holding a cross, a candle (the light of faith) or other source of light, and sometimes a bible. Other symbolic objects in the painting may include the baptismal **font (459)**, used in Christian initiation rituals, and the **chalice (460)**, a symbol of the sanctified wine that represents the redemptive blood of Christ.

461   CROSS

The cross is not only the most important emblem of the Christian faith but also the most famous of all geometric symbols. It has many meanings in general symbolism, notably as the ancient sign of the elemental gods who were thought to rule the four directions of space. Veneration of wind and rain gods accounts for the ritual use of crosses by pagan South American tribes, a discovery that baffled early missionaries. In Hinduism, crossed sticks can symbolize the Vedic fire god, Agni – one of the tradition's principal deities, he is believed to act as a mediator between the mortal and divine worlds.

In early Christianity, various objects were used as a **crux dissimulata (462),** or disguised cross, in order to lessen the risk of persecution. These included the anchor (a sign still found on some church porticos), swastika, axe and trident. In terms of attracting new converts, the cross itself did not

PANDORA·OPENS·THE·BOX

in any case seem an auspicious symbol because of its grim connection with the punishment of criminals and political agitators. Constantine, the first Christian Emperor of Rome, preferred to march under the sign of the **Chi-Rho (463)**, a spoked wheel monogram using the first two Greek letters of the name Christ (XP) with the P superimposed on the X. This sign, close in form to ancient emblems of sun gods, appeared to him in a vision and probably reflected his belief that Jesus was a new incarnation of the sun. The traditional cross of faith is the **crux immissa (464)** with a bar crossing the shaft high up, but Jesus may have died on a T-shaped cross.

465   HOPE PERSONIFIED

The figure of Hope in sacred art is often seen alongside Faith because the two are interlinked in meaning – the expectation of eternal life. Hope may be winged or reach up for a crown – both are emblems of aspiration. Nautical elements suggest mariners' hopes of safe harbour. Hope may wear a hat in the form of a ship and stand by an anchor, recalling St Paul's analogy between it and the Christian hope of salvation.

  In mythology, the most famous and mysterious depiction of hope appears in Hesiod's account of how the beautiful but foolish **Pandora (466)** released evils and miseries into the world by opening the lid of the box in which Zeus had enclosed them, and which he had instructed her never to open. The frail, winged figure of Hope alone remained inside, trapped below the lid. Despite its ambiguity (Hope's inclusion as an evil in the box), the story has been interpreted as symbolizing the idea that hope is often humanity's only comfort.

467 GREEN

Green is an indication of hope because of its associations with springtime's renewal of life. In Celtic mythology it was the colour of Tir na n'Og, Isle of the Blessed. The emerald, which is the stone of the Pope, is a Christian emblem of both hope and faith.

468 SILVER

The silvery light of the moon is a symbol of hope in the midst of darkness. Similarly, light edging around storm clouds produces the "silver lining" which became synonymous with hope in upbeat songs during the Great Depression of the 1930s.

469 DAWN

Dawn, which heralds the beginning of every new day, inevitably suggests the rebirth of hope and the possibility of making a fresh start. Because it arrives in the east, it is associated with the generally optimistic symbolism of this direction of space. Aurora, the Roman goddess of dawn and the sister of Apollo, is often shown on Baroque painted ceilings as a rosy optimist, scattering flowers while the clouds of the night flee before her chariot, as in Guercino's dramatic *Sala di Aurora* (1621–23).

470 HOLLY

Holly is one of the evergreens used in ancient festivals as an emblem of hope in the darkness of midwinter. This symbolism was given a powerful new charge by Christian analogies between its thorns and red berries and the Passion of Christ. Hence its central place in Christmas decorations.

471 FALCON

Symbols of hope are frequently played off against its opposite, despair; an example of this is the hooded falcon, which in art portrays the hope of liberty. The general symbolism of this bird is focused on its all-seeing eye and freedom of the air.

JUSTICE

472 JUSTICE PERSONIFIED

Statues personifying justice preside in monumental stone over many law courts, usually in the form of a sturdy woman holding a pair of scales in one hand and a sword in the other. These attributes symbolize the combination of balanced judgment and punitive power needed to see that justice is done. The figure may unexpectedly wear a **blindfold (473).** This signifies not that justice is blind, but that appearances can be misleading in deciding where the truth lies.

474 SCALES

The scales of justice often appear in medieval paintings to symbolize a stern final reckoning. In paintings of the Last Judgement, sinners may be shown sitting in a pan tugged

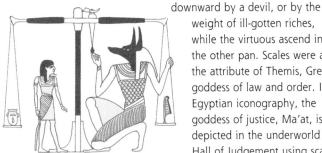

downward by a devil, or by the weight of ill-gotten riches, while the virtuous ascend in the other pan. Scales were also the attribute of Themis, Greek goddess of law and order. In Egyptian iconography, the goddess of justice, Ma'at, is depicted in the underworld Hall of Judgement using scales to weigh the hearts of the dead against an **ostrich feather (475)**. The feather, symbolizing truth, implies that fine judgement is sometimes needed to separate the deserving from the undeserving.

476 COMPASSES

Compasses and other measuring instruments, such as set-squares, are additional attributes of Justice in some paintings. They signify the measured approach of law-makers in this context but were also a popular way for artists to symbolize the difference between spiritual and material values. A famous example is *Newton* by William Blake, who was hostile to science. His painting shows an allegorical figure trying to use a pair of compasses to quantify the universe created by God.

477 LION

Power is very often associated with justice in symbolism. For this reason, and for its aura of pride and dignity, the lion is not only an emblem of the law in India but also appears as the defender of religious law in Buddhism.

See also:

477 Anger and Cruelty, p.248

FORTITUDE AND COURAGE

478   FORTITUDE PERSONIFIED

Fortitude was a popular subject for artists. Its most dramatic personification is a woman, dressed only in a helmet, forcing a lion's jaws apart. Alternatively, she may carry a herculean club and wear a lion skin. A broken pillar refers to the biblical feat in which Samson wrenched a temple down on himself and the Philistines. More conventionally, Gothic sculpture depicts Fortitude in armour. Her symbolism may be emphasized by a contrasting scene in which a knight runs away from a hare – a medieval symbol of cowardice.

See also:

482 Anger and Cruelty, p.248; Peace and Freedom, p.268

484 Femininity and Maternity, p.126

485 Lust, p.243

79–80 HEROES AND HEROINES

Courage is conventionally personified by legends and sagas whose **heroes (479)** and **heroines (480)** either feel no fear or else triumph by overcoming it. To Jungian psychologists, these stories can be read as each individual's journey of self-discovery, a way of readying the human spirit to face the emotional challenges of growing up.

481 ANIMALS

Fierce or powerful wild animals dominate the symbolic representation of courage. Chief among them is the **lion (482)**, even when it is shown as an adversary. In the magnificent relief sculptures created more than 2,500 years ago for palace walls in the Assyrian capital, Ninevah, the lion became the ritual opponent of the king, who is shown in fearless combat with it. Human and lion courage is sometimes matched in images where the king grasps the lion's paws. The lion was the emblematic animal of courage almost everywhere it was known, hence the lion or hybrid-lion statues built to guard shrines. The chow-faced **Karashishi (483)** that guard Buddhist temples in Japan were modelled on second-hand descriptions of lions.

The **bear (484)** and **boar (485)** are both warrior symbols of courage, the boar's ferocity evoking reverence as well as fear. It is associated with warlike divinities such as Wodan, Mars and the Japanese god of war, Hachiman. In Indian mythology, Vishnu in the guise of a heroic boar dives into an abyssal deep to recapture the earth from demons. The **wolf (486)** also has totemic hero symbolism, especially in central Asia. Kemal Atatürk, whose resolute leadership held the Gallipoli Peninsula for Turkey in World War I, was known as the Grey Wolf. Birds that symbolize courage include the **cock (487)**, sacred to the warlike deities Ares and Athene in Greece, and exemplar of military merit and courage in China. Another is the **quail (488)**, a pugnacious bird whose reddish hues linked it with war and valour in China and Rome. In Japan, the **carp (489)** had similar meaning and because it meets death calmly, was associated with the samurai virtue of imperturbability.

See also:

486 Evil, p.162

490 HORN

The virility symbolism of the horn made it an emblem of courage. Horned headdresses in North America were worn only by braves who had distinguished themselves. In Rome, a horned decoration called the **corniculum (491)** had similar meaning and was awarded, as medals are now, for gallantry above the norm.

492 TREES

Trees considered to have unusual strength and resolution were also taken as symbols of courage – notably, the **pine (493)** in China, Japan and Scandinavia. The **oak (494)** was sacred in Europe to gods of war and thunder, such as Odin and Wodan. Its history as an emblem of fortitude lies behind the American oak-leaf cluster military insignia. Some hardy shrubs can have this meaning too – the **camellia (495)** in China, for instance. It blooms in winter as well as summer.

496 STONES AND AMULETS

The hardness of granite and other stones inevitably suggested fortitude. In folk tradition and in gemstone lore, agate, cornelian, jade, ruby and turquoise all symbolize courage. In China, ancient semantic links between "tiger" and amber made this fossil resin a warrior's amulet against fear.

497 NINE

Shamans seem to have used nine as a ritual number associated with male courage or endurance. It was regarded as the strongest yang number in China, probably because it was a triple triad. In a Nordic resurrection myth, the hero-god Odin deliberately wounds and hangs himself for nine days on the World Tree, Yggdrasil, before freeing himself.

TEMPERANCE AND HUMILITY

498 TEMPERANCE PERSONIFIED

The Greek philosophers who made temperance a Cardinal
Virtue were thinking more of moderation than abstinence
from alcohol. This accounts for the different personifications
used to depict this virtue in art. One is a young woman holding or biting a **bridle (499)** – reining herself in. The other is
a woman pouring liquid from one jar to another – substituting water for wine, as Puritan morality would recommend.
The irony that Jesus worked a miracle to achieve the opposite
effect seems to have been missed. In some portraits, artists
suggested the nature of the sitter by posing them with a
clock (500), symbolizing their even temper.

501 VIOLET

This shade is linked both with sobriety and with moderation
in general, a symbolism based on the idea that it is midway
on the spectrum between the red of passion and the blue
of intellectualism. The Roman custom of wearing cooling
wreaths of violets at banquets may have influenced this perception. There were Greek precedents, judging by the name
given to the quartz gemstone **amethyst (502)**,
which literally means "not intoxicated". Its tem-
perate violet or cool purple hue made it the
stone of bishops.

See also:

500 Mortality and
Transience, p.37

Violet is also a colour of humility, one of the lesser virtues, and of modesty or meekness. Violets sometimes surround paintings of Mary and Jesus with this meaning.

503–4 BROWN AND SAFFRON

Brown (503) is associated with both humility and renunciation in the robes of several Christian orders of monks. The same meaning is attached to the **saffron (504)** robes of Buddhist monks. Reputedly, Gautama Buddha adopted this hue when he gave up a secular life of luxury to seek enlightenment in the outside world. Because the colour was worn by criminals at the time, it symbolized not only the Buddha's humility, but also his voluntary separation from materialist society.

505 ASHES

Ashes have been used as a symbol of abasement, worthlessness or humility since ancient times, representing in both the Old and New Testaments the idea that human life is as nothing before the majesty of God. With different shades of meaning, this symbolism can be seen in the customs by which ashes were mixed with food or, as they still are in India, daubed on the body by yogis to

See also:

505 Rebirth and Resurrection, p.335

See also:
507 Power, p.90
510 Lust, p.243

show the low value of human existence.
Sackcloth and ashes were worn in Judah to
signify humility as well as penitence.

506 BARE FEET

The closely linked ideas of humility and abasement can
also be seen in the custom of some mendicant monks going
barefoot. The same theme is revealed in the story of Christ
washing the feet of his disciples. This symbolic gesture was
imitated by some pious English monarchs who washed the
feet of the poor.

507 SHAVED HEAD

Although its symbolism today is often different, shaving the
top of the scalp was once a symbol of humility, renunciation
and submission in many religious orders. It dated back at
least to priestly customs in ancient Egypt as a way both of
marking out a sacred caste and of signalling rejection of personal power, with which abundant hair was closely linked.

508 BEGGING BOWL

The begging bowl is an important symbol of humility and
piety in Buddhist countries, particularly in Thailand, where
some young men undertake a period of travel and begging

for spiritual reasons. In South East Asia, Buddhist monks still observe the ancient tradition of the daily begging round whereby they leave their monasteries each morning to beg their food for the day. Several Christian saints are depicted in art carrying begging bowls.

509 JOINED PALMS

In prayer, joined palms traditionally signify the hope of union with God, hence the steeple form pointing upward. But when they are held on the breast, as in the Buddhist custom of greeting, they symbolize humility as well as friendship.

510–11 DONKEY AND LAMB

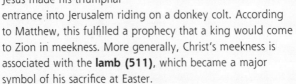

In Western tradition, the **donkey (510)** became the most celebrated animal symbol of humility because three of the gospel writers report that Jesus made his triumphal entrance into Jerusalem riding on a donkey colt. According to Matthew, this fulfilled a prophecy that a king would come to Zion in meekness. More generally, Christ's meekness is associated with the **lamb (511)**, which became a major symbol of his sacrifice at Easter.

GLUTTONY, SLOTH, AVARICE AND PRIDE

512 AVARICE PERSONIFIED

Cupidity and money hoarding were sins particularly condemned by the medieval Church at a time when the poor were numerous and the Church itself was constantly pressuring the rich for more funds. In Gothic sculpture, the personification of avarice was a woman or man clutching a purse or wearing one round the neck. A blindfold symbolized a selfish refusal to see the needs of other people. In some Renaissance paintings of The Last Judgement, vengeful harpies set upon the figure of Avarice, who is shown hoarding emblems of wealth such as golden apples, or money itself.

513 ANIMALS

Moralizing allegories of fleshly appetites or weaknesses used animals as scapegoat symbols. The unfortunate **pig (514)** was chosen by medieval artists to personify gluttony, sloth and lust, three of the **Seven Deadly Sins (515)**. Together with avarice, anger, pride and envy, these collectively symbolized not the worst possible sins of humankind, but venial faults and failings targeted by the Christian Church.

Whereas the sow had widespread positive symbolism in the pagan world, the pig was declared an unclean scavenger in

See also:

515 Protection, p.33

519 Sovereignty, p.103; Vigilance and Guardianship, p.140; Immortality and Eternity, p.329

Judaism and Islam. Christianity largely followed this negative view, especially since pigs were stigmatized in the story of Jesus casting demons into Gadarene swine – read as a warning against sensual greed. Hence the portrayal of a gross pig or man in allegorical scenes of gluttony. This vice could also be represented by the **hedgehog (516)** because of its destructive feeding habits. These included rolling on grapes and carrying them off on its quills. Other animals associated with gluttony in Christian symbolism were the bear, fox and wolf. Portrayals of sloth used either the wallowing pig or the creeping **snail (517)**. Human personifications of this sin show a man riding on a plodding donkey or ox.

518 PRIDE PERSONIFIED

This was another popular subject for medieval artists, who were able to pair the figure of Pride with the most famous emblem of this vice, the **peacock (519)**. Famed in India and Iran, this bird was exhibited as a star turn in other lands of the ancient world, attracting many legends to itself. But for the 2nd-century writer of the Christian text *Physiologus*, the male bird flaunting its resplendent tail was a suitable metaphor for human vanity and arrogance, a haughty creature at odds with Christian concepts of humility.

520 FALLEN ANGEL

In Christian teaching, pride was personified by Satan because it was for this sin that God cast him down with other fallen angels who were his followers. This lesson could be used, as the prophet Isaiah used it, to criticize the arrogance of rulers.

See also:

523 Goodness and Benevolent Power, p.147; Prudence and Wisdom, p.205

521 FALLEN HORSEMAN

Because the mastered horse was an emblem of power, an unseated horseman suggested pride brought low, fulfilling the biblical proverb "pride goes before destruction and a haughty spirit before a fall". In his great painting *The Conversion of St Paul*, Caravaggio drew from medieval allegories on this theme. He shows Saul (as he was called) flat on his back beneath the hoofs of a horse, toppled from his role as a persecutor of Christians by the blinding light of God.

522–3 APE AND MIRROR

Human vanity was sometimes satirized by images of an **ape (522)** holding a **mirror (523)**, or of a woman gazing at her reflection with devils shown in the background. More often, the mirrors that appear in portraits of women are symbols of the ephemeral nature of beauty rather than of pride.

524 TOWER OF BABEL

The stepped temples or ziggurats built by the Babylonians symbolized ascension towards God, an ambition regarded by the Hebrews as presumptuous. Hence the story in Genesis of God disrupting the heavenward progress of the Tower of Babel (see below) by causing its workforce to speak so many different languages that confusion reigned and the project failed. The story is usually taken as an allegory of human pride and arrogance.

CHASTITY AND VIRGINITY

525 CHASTITY PERSONIFIED

The wide range of symbols for chastity reflects the importance placed on it in male-dominated societies before the age of birth control. This was true even before Christianity made it a key feminine virtue, and also a masculine one for men entering monastic orders. In medieval sacred art, chastity is usually personified by a veiled woman carrying a shield to rebuff desire or deflect the arrows of Cupid. She may sometimes be seen trampling a pig or boar representing bestial lusts.

526 PAGAN VIRGINS

The Greek Artemis and her Roman counterpart, Diana, were virgin goddesses linked with night hunting, and therefore with the moon, whose **crescent (527)** they are sometimes shown wearing in their hair – the moon itself was an emblem of chastity in secular and sacred art. They both appear with this meaning in classical allegories of desire and restraint. **Silver (528)** became an emblem of chastity because it was associated with moonlight. Another often depicted symbol of chastity is the nymph **Daphne (529)**, shown being turned into a laurel tree to protect her from the lust of Apollo, as in the virtuoso marble statue by Bernini in the Borghese Gallery, Rome.

530 CELIBATES

Religious celibates represent a sacrificial form of chastity. Rome's **Vestal Virgins (531)**, who guarded the city's sacred fire under the protection of the goddess of the hearth, Vesta, were punished by a slow death if they transgressed the vows they had taken. They remain the most famous group of female celibates, although many other pagan priestesses took vows of virginity, including those who served the sun god in Peru. Among male celibates celebrated in art the best-known is **St Anthony (532)**. A tongue-in-cheek picture by Watteau shows him praying to be delivered from his lust when a group of seductive women visit him in his hermit cave.

533 VIRGIN MOTHERS

Virgin motherhood symbolizes the birth of an extraordinary being – one whose nature has, by inference, some admixture of the divine. Countless myths and legends in which exceptional men or women are fathered by gods upon a virginal human mother testify to the power of this concept. They include Romulus and Remus, whose father was said to be the god of war, Mars. The Roman Catholic doctrine of the **Immaculate Conception (534)** took this a stage further in asserting that the Virgin Mary was herself born to a

See also:

528 Faith and Hope, p.178

virgin mother, Anne. The implication of Anne's own chastity is that Mary was untouched by Original Sin when she conceived Jesus.

The enormous cult of the **Madonna (535)** has made her the most notable representative of chastity in Western art, and she is often depicted with other emblems of this Christian virtue.

536 UNICORN

The most poetic animal symbol of chastity is the unicorn, a fabulous hybrid with a spiral horn on its forehead which appears with a young woman in many medieval paintings and tapestries. According to legend, the unicorn could be captured only by a virgin – perhaps a reference back to the virgin huntresses of classical myth. With her, the beast would become meek and lay its horn in her lap. In other words, a pure woman could tame the horn of male desire. The image is one of both male and female chastity, the virtuous sweetness of unconsummated love.

In sacred art where the unicorn is seen with the Virgin Mary the image takes on a spiritual dimension, the creature's spiral horn symbolizing the penetration of her body by the Holy Spirit. The figure of Chastity is sometimes shown in art riding in a chariot pulled by unicorns.

537 LILY

In sacred art, female saints, and some
male ones, are shown with a lily,
in this context an emblem of both
purity and chastity. It can also be
seen in paintings of the Annunciation where it is either
held by the archangel Gabriel or set in a vase beside the
figure of Mary. She was the medieval "lily among thorns".

538 ALMOND

The almond has ancient associations with the idea of self-
generation because the juice from pressed almonds was
linked with semen. Hence old European superstitions that
virgins could wake up pregnant if they fell asleep under an
almond tree. In classical mythology, Attis, beloved by the
earth goddess Cybele, was said to have sprung from an
almond, and the biblical story of Aaron's rod appears to
use the same symbolism. Aaron, head of the house of Levi,
showed his right to lead the Israelite priesthood when his
rod miraculously blossomed and produced almonds. It is at
least possible that these traditions influenced the form of the
mandorla (539), an almond-shaped frame which symbolizes
both virgin birth and the Ascension when it encloses Jesus
and Mary in Christian art.

540–2 EARLY FLOWERING PLANTS

A number of spring-flowering plants were once symbols of virginity through their association with youth. **Peach blossom (540)** was an emblem of virginity in both Japan and China. In ancient Rome, brides carried or wore **olive leaves (541)** as symbols of chastity. And **hawthorn (542)** was also used in Roman bridal garlands. Later folk tradition in Europe claimed that hawthorn could be used to protect chastity.

543 THE CHASTE ELEPHANT

An unexpected symbol of male celibacy is the elephant. This curious association arose in medieval times, when bestiaries (books of animal allegories) praised the chastity of the bull elephant during the long gestation period of his mate, which can extend to 22 months.

544 ERMINE

A legend that ermine (mammals also known as stoats and weasels) died if their white winter coat was soiled led to ermine becoming another symbol for chastity. Leonardo da Vinci was one of several Renaissance painters to pose a young woman with ermine to denote her purity.

545 DOVE

Like many Christian emblems, the depiction of the figure of Chastity with a pair of turtle doves is at odds with classical symbolism. The Greeks and Romans would have read sensual love into such an image. Medieval artists, however, were told by bestiaries of the day that doves mated for life, and as a result they chose them to represent chastity in the sense of marital fidelity.

546 JEWELS

The idea of virginity as having a high value led to pale or white gemstones becoming emblems of chastity, notably the **pearl (547)**. An ancient belief that oysters produced pearls through a process of celestial impregnation linked the pearl with virgin conception in the womb of Mary. Other chastity

See also:

545 Femininity and Maternity, p.129

547 Love, p.232

549 Love, p.231

550 Gluttony, Sloth, Avarice and Pride, p.195

stones include the **crystal (548)** for its flaw-less clarity and the **diamond (549)** for its association with virtue.

550–1 TOWER AND CASTLE

In literature and art, the image of a woman in a **tower (550)** or barricaded in a **castle (551)** is an archetypal sym-bol of protected virginity. In Spain, a grill-like emblem of crossed bars depicted the same idea in summary form. Medieval paintings sometimes show a personification of Chastity at a tower window or behind a castle para-pet. More playful allegories on the theme of love show young women on the battlements defending their chastity while youths attack the castle with flowers or fruit.

552 MIRROR

Looking glasses in myth and legend are usually linked with women, and early mirrors of polished metal were attributes of several mother goddesses.

However, the symbolism of virginity is specific in pictures that show the Madonna holding a mirror. Here the reference is to the apocryphal Book of Wisdom, which refers to Mary as the "mirror without stain", a flawless reflection of God's goodness.

553 GARDEN

Late-medieval artists often showed the Virgin Mary sitting in a garden which included bordering walls or hedges of roses or other thorny plants. The image was taken from the Song of Solomon which, in the monkish imagination of Bernard of Clairvaux, was an allegory of Jesus and his virgin mother. One of its verses reads: "A garden enclosed is my sister, my spouse; a spring shut up, a fountain sealed". This is the symbolic significance of paintings that depict the Annunciation taking place in a garden, or which show Mary with the infant Jesus in such a setting.

See also:

553 Fecundity and Plenty, p.57

555 Evil, p.155

557 Salvation and Redemption, p.318

PRUDENCE AND WISDOM

554 PRUDENCE PERSONIFIED

Greek philosophers made prudence one of the Cardinal
Virtues because the word implied for them not caution so
much as wise foresight. Because the **snake (555)** was an
ancient emblem of wisdom, it is shown in art entwining the
female figure of Prudence – an image that can easily be
misread in view of other snake symbolism. Prudence may
also hold a **mirror (556)** which, in this context, stands for
self-knowledge.

557 ANCHOR

The anchor is another attribute sometimes shown with the figure of Prudence.
The meaning here is that it makes
sense to stop and think before acting. A famous motto of the Roman
Emperor Augustus was *festina lente*
(hasten slowly). Renaissance artists
illustrated this with the motif of a dolphin
(speed) twined round an anchor (restraint).

558 WISDOM PERSONIFIED

In Gothic art, the female figure of Wisdom is almost inter-
changeable with that of Prudence, although she is more

often shown holding a book. Renaissance artists looked back to classical mythology in which the militant goddess Athene (the Roman Minerva) represented wisdom. Therefore, Wisdom appears as a physical and mental warrior, helmeted and wearing armour and confusingly holding both a shield and an olive branch. The olive was linked with a celebrated myth involving another attribute of Wisdom, the owl.

559–61 OLIVE AND OWL

Athens was named for the goddess Athene because, according to legend, she won a contest for the city's patronage by inventing the olive tree. This miraculous sign of her intelligence and foresight associated not only the **olive (559)** with wisdom but also the **owl (560)**, which was said to be her companion. Athens adopted the owl as its emblem, and put it on the reverse side of coins carrying Athene's image. Because of its association with the centre of Greek civilization, and with Athene herself, the owl entered European fable as the wisest of all birds and with this meaning would later become a common motif on book covers. **Birds (561)** in general were widely linked with speed of thought and with wisdom in the sense of wide knowledge. Hence the expression "a little bird told me".

See also:

560 Evil, p.160

562 Evil, p.155;
Envy and Jealousy,
p.245

562 SERPENT

As goddess of wisdom, Athene was also associated with the serpent. Her sacred snake was kept in one of her temples, the Erechtheum in Athens. Temple snakes were associated with the mysteries of the underworld and with prophetic advice throughout the ancient Middle East – hence, perhaps, the biblical description of the serpent in the garden of Eden as "more crafty than any other wild animal". In the gospel of Matthew, Jesus advises his disciples to be "wise as serpents" in carrying his message to the lost sheep of the house of Israel.

563–4 BABOON AND IBIS

Among the more puzzling aspects of Egyptian iconography is the depiction of Thoth, god of wisdom, learning and creativity, as a **baboon (563)**. He is also represented in the form of an **ibis (564)**. Both bird and beast have been found mummified near Thebes and appear in many carvings. Thoth, probably an ancient lunar god, was worshipped as the omniscient inventor of both science and the arts. He was even more famous as the author of all-powerful books of magic. The Greeks called him Hermes Trismegistus (three times great), and he was also known as "The Silent Being", "The Silver Aten" and "Beautiful Night".

565 SPHINX

For some centuries after the
Renaissance the sphinx
became a symbol of
inscrutable wisdom. The
Egyptian Great Sphinx
of Giza, a human-
headed lion seen
by romantic trav-
ellers as embodying
the "wisdom of the ages", was conflated with a riddle-posing
Greek sphinx. This was depicted as a seductive woman with
breasts and wings superimposed on the body of a lioness.
Sophocles' Oedipus is saved from its clutches by answering
the riddle: "What goes on four legs in the morning, two at
midday and three at night?" (A man).

566–7 WATER AND SPRINGS

Water (566) is a Taoist metaphor for wisdom, finding its
way around obstacles by subtle means rather than by force.
In the myths of many lands are **springs (567)** or fountains
of wisdom, rising inexhaustibly from the depths of the earth,
conferring secret knowledge on those who drink from them.
Odin, the Scandinavian and Teutonic god of wisdom, was so

thirsty for knowledge that he gave one of his eyes to his uncle, Mimir, in return for a draught from the fountain of wisdom beneath the World Tree. The symbolic links between water and wisdom, in the sense of revealed knowledge, is particularly widespread in Celtic legend and folklore.

568 SALMON

Irish and Welsh legends of a "salmon of wisdom" make a poetic analogy between the difficult winning of knowledge and the resolute struggle of the salmon to reach its spawning grounds. Symbolic associations between water and fish strengthen tales in which Celtic heroes gain knowledge from the fish. In the legend of Finn mac Cumhaill he acquires his remarkable mental powers accidentally when he burns his thumb on a magic

salmon that he has allowed to overcook. The gift of
prophecy falls on him the moment he puts his thumb
into his mouth to sooth it.

569 NUT-BEARING TREES

Celtic tales of wise salmon mention
that the fish feed on hazel nuts
dropped into the water from the
Tree of Knowledge. The hazel is
only one of many trees whose
fruit supposedly conferred
wisdom or prophetic powers.
Acorns, almonds and walnuts
have also suggested the symbolism of hidden truth lying within a
hard outer casing.

570–1 SEVEN AND THREE

The mystic number **seven (570)** is often linked with intellect
and wisdom, a symbolism thought to be based on the implication of progression and accomplishment in the seven days
of the week. Hence, perhaps, the verse in the Book of
Proverbs which says the house of wisdom has seven pillars.
In Buddhist iconography, the Buddha's footprint bears seven

symbols of his divine wisdom, and the Buddha is said to have taken seven paces along each cardinal direction of space in order to comprehend the entire universe.

For Pythagoras, who linked wisdom with harmony, the significant number was **three (571)**; Pythagoreans used the triangle as a sign for wisdom and associated it with the goddess of this virtue, Athene.

572–3 EYE AND HEART

An **eye (572)** in a palm is a Buddhist emblem of compassionate wisdom. The "Third Eye" of Hinduism represents the transcendent wisdom of the **heart (573)**. Symbolically, these ideas reflect ancient traditions in which there is no rigid division between heart and head in terms of knowledge and understanding – wisdom is not considered simply as a product of the brain. The 17th-century French philosopher Blaise Pascal put it not too differently in writing: "The heart has its reasons which reason knows nothing of".

See also:

570 Protection, p.33

571 Fame and Fortune, p.72

572 Vigilance and Guardianship, p.140

FIDELITY AND LOYALTY

574 FIDELITY PERSONIFIED

The virtue personified in art is not marital loyalty but the trustworthiness of a servant. This explains why Fidelity appears as a woman holding a key and a golden seal. A much more popular symbol of fidelity is the dog which sometimes accompanies her.

575 DOG

The dog's emblematic association with loyalty was greatly strengthened during the 19th century, when illustrators and painters such as Landseer capitalized on Victorian sentimentalism with heart-wrenching pictures of dogs sitting beside graves, "faithful unto death". This is also the significance of medieval statuary in which dogs are shown lying at the feet of entombed masters or mistresses.

There are ancient precedents for this symbolism in many cultures where dogs were guardians, companions and guides in death as well as in life. In Celtic tradition, they are companions of warriors, hunters and goddesses of health. Legends of several Christian saints associate the dog with devoted care and companionship. It is one emblem of the clergy, and appears as a faithful guardian in allegories of the Good Shepherd.

576 KNIGHT

Loyalty and honourable service were pre-requisites of knighthood, and the symbolism of fidelity underlies the countless depictions of knights in art, literature and legend, even though a range of other moral virtues were added to their image. The unbreakable vow, the willingness to meet any danger even at the cost of his own life, was an inherent part of the knight's larger symbolism as a perfected medieval warrior for lord, lady or God.

577-8 GIRDLE AND RING

The binding implication of the **girdle (577)** made it an ancient emblem of fidelity to vows, marital or spiritual, in much the same way as a **ring (578)** does. Roman soldiers laid aside their girdle (a weapon belt) as a symbolic gesture when they left the service, and Roman women were given a woollen girdle as an emblem of bridal fidelity. The rope girdle worn by Franciscan monks signified not only the binding and scourging of Christ but also their own vows of service to him. Three knots tied in it stood for obedience, chastity and poverty.

579 STONE
According to gemstone lore, the diamond, emerald, garnet, hyacinth, opal and topaz are all traditional fidelity emblems, but any precious stone shares the general symbolism of permanence that attaches to stone itself.

580 DUCK
Duck motifs are sometimes used in Chinese wedding décor as emblems of fidelity. The symbolism is drawn from the habits of mandarin ducks, who often pair off and swim in perfectly synchronized patterns.

581 CRANE
The crane is a major emblem of fidelity in China. Contributing to this symbolism are its impressive mating dance, its constant migrational reappearances in winter and its reputation throughout Asia for longevity.

582 ROSEMARY
The lingering fragrance of this herb may account for its use in Roman marriage ceremonies as a token of faithful love. Its Latin name *ros marinus*, meaning "sea dew", linked it with the love goddess, Venus, who was born from sea foam. An echo of these ancient associations can be heard in Shakespeare's

distraught Ophelia, who reproaches Hamlet: "There's rose-mary, that's for remembrance; pray you, love, remember."

583 IVY

Ivy is another plant some-times used as an emblem of fidelity, particularly in Christian art, not only because it clings, but also because it is an evergreen. It is also, of course, a sign of time passing. The Victorian narrative artist, Arthur Hughes, used both these symbolic aspects in his painting *The Long Engagement*. It shows a clergyman, who cannot afford to marry, standing with his patient fiancée near a tree on which ivy threatens to obliterate the names they carved into it in the first flush of love.

PURITY AND INCORRUPTIBILITY

584   WHITE

As the purest of all hues, white represents the pure conscience, clear of stain, a symbolism used in both the Christian and Islamic worlds. It signifies purity not only in the conventions of white weddings, white knights and white-robed priests, but also in the tradition of candidates to mystery sects wearing white to show the purity of their motives. The word candidate itself comes from the Latin for "shining white".

The whiteness of **milk (585)** made it, too, an emblem of purity. In legends of Church martyrs, St Catherine of Alexandria was said to have shed milk rather than blood when she was decapitated.

> **See also:**
>
> **584** Defeat, Cowardice and Betrayal, p.280
> **586** Fertility, p.54

586   LILY

Although the lily often signifies female chastity in Christian art, its more general symbolism is purity. Thus, although the white lily named "Madonna" is the flower of the Virgin Mary, it is also associated with her husband, Joseph, and others. This is in spite of older traditions in which it had erotic and fecundity significance. A factor in its Christian symbolism are the verses of Matthew in which Jesus asks his disciples to consider the lilies of the field, and says: "even Solomon in all his glory was not arrayed like one of these".

587 FIRE

Fire is more an agent of purification – the burning away of impurities – than an emblem of purity itself. But a flame can symbolize the force of purity, as in the biblical image of cherubim with flaming swords who bar a human

return to the Garden of Eden. The Holy Spirit is equated with fire, and Jehovah spoke from the fire of a mountain and from the heart of a burning bush.

588   WATER

Water has always had both general and specific purity symbolism. Emblematically, its freshest form is **dew (589)**, reputedly the nectar of the immortals. It was associated in Hinduism with the divine word, and in Christianity with the Holy Spirit. In Chinese mythology, a Tree of Sweet Dew grew at the centre of the world. A similar theme in Christianity is the concept of a **spring (590)** of purity and salvation issuing at the roots of the Tree of Life and flowing out through the four streams of paradise. Belief in the unpolluted purity of mineral springs played a part in the miraculous cures they were credited with achieving. But even village ponds shared in the purity symbolism of water. It was for this reason that women accused of witchcraft were sometimes thrown into them. Their persecutors argued that when they came to the surface, as most did, the water was rejecting them as impure.

591   DEER

The image of deer sipping water from pools or lakes poetically linked them with both purity and piety. They appear with this symbolism in medieval sacred art. A hart was the emblem of Charles VI of France to whom, according to popular legend, a stag had knelt as he entered Rouen. In the Wilton Diptych, a **white hart (592)** is worn on the breast of Richard II of England and is also a motif on the robes of angels attending the Virgin Mary and Jesus.

593 HONEY

Honey drew its celestial symbolism not only from its wonderful golden colour but also from ancient beliefs that it was a food that was free of impurity. This seems to have been based on the idea that bees made honey not from collecting pollen but by sipping pure dew from flowers. The scholar-poet Samuel Coleridge used this image in the marvellous closing lines of *Kubla Khan*: "For he on honeydew hath fed/and drunk the milk of Paradise".

594 INCENSE

Scented resins such as gum were burnt as incense from ancient times as symbols of both purity and incorruptibility in religious, sacrificial or funerary rites. Resin was also used in embalming because it was thought to be the incorruptible essence of trees.

595–8 IVORY, GOLD AND PRECIOUS STONES

The whiteness of **ivory (595)** partially accounts for its Christian symbolism of purity, but the material has much older links with incorruptibility. It was used for carving small magical amulets or sacred objects for thousands of years before it became the preferred medium of carving in the monastic workshops of the 9th and 10th centuries, during the Carolingian renaissance of art.

In China, both ivory and **jade (596)** represented moral purity and incorruptibility in the official life and administration of the empire. Tablets and pendants of ivory marked high office, and jade insignia was used in both court ceremony and religious ritual. The connection between jade and incorruptibility led to the medicinal use of powdered jade in an attempt to prolong life. For the same emblematic reason, jade amulets were sometimes buried with the dead. In Western tradition, **gold (597)** has similar associations because of its solar colour and resistance to rust. It was the metal of ultimate purity in alchemy. Among precious stones, its purity symbolism is matched only by the **diamond (598)**, which in India is equated with the Philosopher's Stone of alchemy and which has become a Western metaphor for shining probity.

599 SALT

Because of its preservative uses, salt was an ancient symbol of incorruptibility and of an unbreakable covenant in the Semitic world. The Book of Leviticus made salt an obligatory offering to be given with all Hebrew meat sacrifices as they were the salt (pure and unchanging intent) of God's covenant with his people. Jesus called his disciples the pure "salt of the earth". Salt was also a key symbol of good faith in the Arab world and an emblem of purity in Greek and Roman tradition. Its symbolism of incorruptibility led some mourners to put salt into coffins.

See also:

596 Health, p.82; Authority, p.101

597 Wealth and Prosperity, p.66

Emotions and Instincts

Love 224

Lust 240

Envy and Jealousy 244

Anger and Cruelty 247

Happiness and Joy 250

Grief, Mourning and
Melancholia. 254

Instinct, Intuition and
the Unconscious 260

LOVE

600 LOVE PERSONIFIED

In Western art, Venus and Cupid have been the most famous personifications of love since the 15th century when Renaissance painters and sculptors began to illustrate classical mythology. **Venus (601)** was based on the Greek goddess Aphrodite who, according to the poet Hesiod, symbolized "the sweet pleasure and gentle delicacy of love". Later stories of her projected a passionate and sensual image, and the Venus of Roman myth and art more often symbolizes sensual than spiritual love. Titian's painting *Sacred and Profane Love* illustrates the dichotomy by showing two Venuses, one a worldly seductress, fashionably dressed, the other divinely naked and holding up a flame – emblem of a loftier ideal of love.

The Roman god of love, **Cupid (602)**, also evolved from Grecian models. Hesiod's original god Eros symbolized the transforming power of desire. Plato spiritualized his image by suggesting that true love lies beyond mere sexual appetite. The figure of Cupid is different. He more often symbolizes infatuation – sudden, amoral and often short-lived. His **bow and arrows (603)** stand for love's wounds and his **blindfold (604)** for love's blindness and its randomly aimed darts. In paintings that illustrate the conquest of love, Cupid may play a more elevated role and be seen overcoming lust.

605 HEART

The heart is today almost a synonym for love, universally recognized in its sentimental, stylized form, tapering downwards from a swelling upper lip. But the use of a heart

See also:

605 Prudence and Wisdom, p.211

as a symbol of romantic ardour may date back no earlier than the Middle Ages. In the ancient world, the heart was predominately a philosophical symbol of the centre. It gradually evolved into a symbol of love as the emotion of love itself moved towards the centre of spiritual and sensual life.

A flaming heart can symbolize the religious devotion of saints or mystics and also the devotion of a man to a woman, or vice-versa. Similarly, the image of a heart transfixed by an arrow can symbolize the love and suffering of Jesus or, in the context of St Valentine's day, sensual longing or undying love. For Catholics, the "Sacred Heart", pierced with nails or crowned with thorns, became a key emblem of the Counter-Reformation. It represented Christ's redeeming love.

Psychologically, the heart is a feminine symbol because of its vase-like, containing shape. The **vase (606)** can itself represent the loving heart when it is decorated by the motif of a man and a woman holding hands.

607 MUSICAL INSTRUMENTS

Musical instruments are frequently associated with gods of
love, and it was the troubadour poet-musicians of medieval
Provence who first established the Western romantic concept
of love. The young Mozart sent coded letters to an "English
rose" in which musical notes were substituted for letters of
the alphabet. Music's power to stir, celebrate and renew love
underlies the Greek myth of **Orpheus (608)** which symbolizes
the human belief that love can conquer even death. Carrying
only his **lyre (609)**, he follows his dead wife to the underworld and sings so passionately of his enduring love that
Death relents and Eurydice almost escapes to rejoin the living.

The **flute (610)** has more obvious sexual symbolism. It is
the instrument of the Indian love god **Krishna (611)** who

was said to have brought the world into existence by playing it, and who uses it to seduce an entire group of *gopis* (daughters and wives of cow-herders), among them his beloved, the goddess Radha. The flute – an instrument also of the great god **Pan (612)**, a Greek symbol of free and natural love – appears often in the sensual etchings of Picasso.

The **lute (613)** was the most popular emblem of romantic love in Renaissance art and is the instrument most often seen in paintings as an attribute of Cupid.

614   FLOWERS

Flowers have been tokens of both spiritual and sensual love for centuries, and still are in modern lovers' bouquets and Valentines – their powerful symbolism is drawn from ancient association with beauty, youth and joy. Even the word **posy (615)** is itself symbolic because it derives from "poesy", meaning a poem or motto of love. Flowers have remained the most popular messengers of love, partly because they capture its fresh spontaneity. But the Victorians worked out a more contrived flower code in which selected blooms were used in courtship to convey different shades of meaning. A **yellow rose (616)** could

See also:

614 Mortality and Transience, p.36; Grief, Mourning and Melancholia, pp.257–8; Enlightenment and Transformation, p.340

suggest that the sender was jealous of a rival, while a bouquet of **white roses (617)** expressed conventional respect for the youthful purity of the receiver.

The pre-eminent flower of passion is the **red rose (618)**, an ancient emblem of love goddesses, and the attribute, in art, of Venus. The red rose of desire with its wounding thorns has an extraordinary tradition in Western art and literature as a mystic symbol of the heart's tormented quest for perfect union in love. Yet the red rose is also the colour of arousal and a secret genital emblem. The **lotus (619)** is counterpart to the rose in Eastern tradition as an idealized version of the vulva. Indian miniatures sometimes show Krishna presenting the flower to his love, Radha, while in Tantric Buddhism, the stem and blossom of the lotus forms a masculine-feminine image of sexual and spiritual harmony. A **pansy (620)**, with its heart-shaped flowers, expresses love in the sense of fond remembrance. The pansy's name comes from the French word for thought, *pensée*. The **red carnation (621)** was a token of betrothal in Flanders, and it appears in some Netherlandish paintings with this significance.

622 LOCK OF HAIR

Locks of hair have been exchanged by lovers since antiquity and are often the most intimate keepsakes carried by lovers who have had to endure long separations. They symbolize a surrender to love, the giving of an essential part of one's identity to another person.

623 RINGS

The symbolism of the rings given in engagement and marriage is not only union in love but also publicly avowed commitment. Ancient Roman betrothal rings were made in the form of clasped hands, and during the Renaissance hearts or other tiny keepsakes were hidden in the bezels of rings. But usually any added significance is carried by the jewel set into a ring or the material of which it is made. Wedding rings of plain **gold (624)** symbolized enduring love in ancient Celtic custom, and still do. The custom of wearing a wedding ring on the fourth finger originated in the 16th century when physicians claimed that a vein on this finger ran directly to the heart.

625 RED STONES

Symbolic links with the fires of passion made red stones emblems of ardent love. The most notable example is the **ruby (626)**; it was reputed to enflame lovers and to alter its hue if love waned. It was said that Catherine of Aragon's ruby grew paler as Henry VIII transferred his affections to Anne Boleyn. The ruby was linked to marital happiness in China, Japan and Burma. The **red garnet (627)** and the **carbuncle (628)** are similarly linked with passion, but also with war, making them precarious choices as love tokens.

629 DIAMOND

As the most popular of engagement stones, the emblematic meaning of the diamond is lasting love – an important consideration given the frequency of broken engagements. The stone's durability made it a natural choice as a symbol of both sincerity and constancy.

630 SAPPHIRE

Another brilliant engagement stone, the sapphire draws from its celestial blue shade the symbolism of truth, serenity, harmony and

See also:

622 Strength and Stability, p.113; Peace and Freedom, p.271

629 Health, p.83; Chastity and Virginity, p.203

domestic peace – qualities that again suggest the hope of lasting love.

631 PEARL

Connected by its shape and luminosity with the moon, and by its origins with water, the pearl is overwhelmingly feminine in symbolism, ambivalently representing not only purity but also sexuality. Its ancient association with the foam-born goddess of love, Venus, who was said to have worn pearls, adds to its emblematic significance.

632 GARDEN

In Persian, Indian, Asian and European art, lovers are frequently shown in a garden setting. A symbolic link is made in such paintings between the blossoming of love and the sensory delights of the garden – the ideal romantic space for secret meetings, with its flowers, birds, burgeoning plants and bowers.

See also:

631 Bad Luck, p.79; Chastity and Virginity, p.202

One theme of Renaissance garden painting is the **Fountain of Youth (633)**, above which Cupid presides while bathers enter the

water as old people and emerge young and invigorated. The symbolism is that love, like the jetting water, has rejuvenating effects.

634   KNOT

An open knot pattern is a symbol of love's bind-ing union, and sometimes a clandestine emblem of sexual coupling in Renaissance art. Cupid occupies himself in tying a knot in some paintings of Venus with Mars who, in classical myth, cuckolded the love goddess's husband, Vulcan. In Victorian times, "tying the knot" became a synonym for marriage. The motif continues to be popular, sometimes showing paired initials within the knot, or a knot in the form of a bow tie.

635   NIGHTINGALE

The combined emotions of pain and joy that often accom-pany the experience of love are traditionally symbolized by the haunting spring song of the male nightingale. The bird's connection with love and the hurt it can bring is derived from the Greek myth of Philomela, who was raped by her brother-in-law, who then cut out her tongue so that she would be prevented from reporting his crime. The gods turned her into a nightingale, allowing her piteous tale to be told in the music of its song.

See also:

636 Peace and Freedom, p.266

636 DOVE

In modern times, the dove's link with peace has made it an emblem of tender and gentle love. Its ancient symbolism was more overtly sexual, as is shown by Pompeian motifs of doves with a winged phallus. Its moan was associated with sexual pleasure, and doves were companions of the great Middle Eastern goddess of love, Astarte, as well as of several classical gods and goddesses, including both Venus and Cupid. The image of two doves facing each other stands for marital harmony and constancy.

637 PARTRIDGE

The partridge, praised in Iran for its graceful and seductive beauty, was also associated with Mediterranean and Middle Eastern love goddesses, its reddish hues suggesting passion. By association, its flesh was superstitiously thought to be an aphrodisiac.

638 SWAN

In Western poetry, music and ballet, the swan's elegant,
iconic beauty has often been used as a symbol of lost love
or melancholy passion. The classical myth of Zeus using
swan form to ravish Leda itself suggests the passionate rush
of love and its ebbing. The hero of a happier Irish legend
identifies his true love in the form of a swan wearing a gold
neck chain. In Ovid's retelling of
Greek fables, swans draw the
chariot of Venus.

639 DEER

Painful symptoms of love were once thought
to be the expression of an actual physical or
mental illness. This accounts for medieval
images of a deer pierced by an arrow and
carrying herbs in its mouth – an
emblem of lovesickness. Deer had curative symbolism and were thought
to seek and use medicinal herbs.

640 FRUIT

Many fruits have sexual significance, either through their
shapes, seeds or succulent juices, and some were said to
have aphrodisiac powers.

One such fruit was the **tomato (641)**, which was brought
to Europe from South America by the Spanish, who called it
a "love apple". The **pear (642)**, which is another emblem of
love associated with Aphrodite (Venus), undoubtedly owes
its erotic symbolism to its smooth rounded form, strongly
suggestive of the female breasts and pelvis.

Based on the resemblance between
its bisected core and the female genitals,
the **apple (643)** is an ancient emblem
of sexual bliss. This is its meaning in

See also:

643 Immortality
and Eternity, p.326

dreams, according to the Greek writer Artemidorus, one of the first to attempt to classify dream symbols. An apple is the prize Paris awards to Aphrodite (Venus) in the influential myth of Eris (discord) throwing a golden apple amongst the gods marked "to the fairest" and setting off a bitter dispute between rival goddesses. Its widespread use as a symbol of love led to it becoming known as the fruit of temptation in the Garden of Eden – although Genesis does not name it specifically. The **orange (644)**, also an ancient symbol of love, is an alternative to the apple preferred by some artists as the paradisial forbidden fruit.

What Homer called the "honey-sweet fruit" of the **pomegranate (645)** became a symbol for sensual love and its binding power, because in classical myth it was the fruit that drew Persephone (or Proserpina) back to her underworld lord, Hades, after he had forced her to take a bite of it. This is the emblematic meaning of *Proserpina* (1874), a painting by the pre-Raphaelite artist Dante Gabriel Rossetti, in which a beautiful woman holds a bitten pomegranate. The pomegranate is a marriage and fecundity symbol that is linked with mother goddesses as well as love goddesses.

The luscious **strawberry (646)**, with its glorious red flesh and soft, swelling, heart-like shape, appears as a dominant emblem of carnal love in the Gothic art of Hieronymus Bosch. His extraordinary triptych, *The Garden of Earthly Delights* (below), shows couples biting greedily into the fruit, oblivious to the retributive horrors depicted on the following panel, Hell.

LUST

647 LUST PERSONIFIED

Although increasingly acknowledged as a universal emotion, lust was seen by the medieval Church as one of the worst of the Seven Deadly Sins. Its usual personification in art is a naked woman with snakes and toads feeding on her breasts and genitals. The cruelty of this symbolism reflects the Church's particular disapproval of female sexuality. Christian symbology is unique in using snakes and toads as emblems of lust, although they do have widespread fertility symbolism elsewhere. The ape, boar and bear are among several other animals linked by Christianity with the sin of lechery.

648–9 CENTAUR AND HORSE

Male lust is most strikingly symbolized by the **centaur (648)**, an equine hybrid with a man's head, arms and torso superimposed on the body of a horse. Myths of centaurs as lawless and drunken rapists perhaps grew out of tales of the wild activities of horse-riding cow herders. A counter-mythology presented one race of centaurs as healers and teachers. Out of this dichotomy came the centaur familiar in art – an anguished creature struggling to control its baser instincts.

The **horse (649)** is a powerful emblem of lust, or the brute speed and force of sexual

See also:

649 War and Victory, p.277; Death, p.300

desire. In a famous Romantic painting by Fuseli called
The Nightmare, a wall-eyed horse bursts into the bedroom
of a sleeping woman upon whose breast a demon incubus
squats.

650 SATYR

The satyr of Greek fable symbolizes lustful sexual energy
and devil-may-care hedonism. Medieval depictions of the
devil were based largely on the physical appearance of this
amoral creature – a man with
goatish features including hairy
legs, hooves, a tail and long,
pointy ears or horns. In classical
mythology he follows in the
train of pleasure-loving gods
such as Dionysus (the Roman
Bacchus) and Pan (Faunus),
has his way with nymphs and
naiads and hurls himself into
drunken dances.

The male **goat (651)** set the
pattern for this characterization
by its own impressive virility.
Jewish moralists stigmatized its

behaviour as impure, perhaps because they were aware that intimacy with goats was a cultic practice in at least one Egyptian sect. Christianity took the same disapproving view, making the goat a symbol of destructive lust.

652   MINOTAUR

Ancient worship of the bull's virility may lie behind the influential Attic myth of the Minotaur, a bull-headed man shut up by his father in a Cretan labyrinth. According to sagas of the hero Theseus, seven Athenian girls and seven youths were delivered to this monstrous hybrid every year until Theseus succeeded in killing it. The Minotaur is now read as a symbol of repressed lust, a man who thinks like a bull. It was a favourite motif for Picasso, who depicts it as a cheerful creature participating in a consenting orgy – such a representation reveals how the symbolism of the story is still evolving.

See also:

654
Temperance
and Humility
(Donkey), p.191

653–4   PIG AND ASS

Heedless animal passion is also the symbolism of the **pig (653)**. Allegorical Christian paintings sometimes show the personification of Chastity treading on a pig representing lust. Pigs appear as emblems of sensual greed in the Bible and in classical mythology, as in the story of Circe, who turned her suitors into pigs. The **ass (654)** is another animal used in Greco-Roman legends as an emblem of lust, but usually in tales that have a comical twist.

ENVY AND JEALOUSY

655 **ENVY PERSONIFIED**
As one of the Seven Deadly Sins, this common human
failing is most sensationally personified by a woman who
has torn her heart from her breast and is chew-
ing it. Hence the origin of the expression "eat
your heart out".

656–8 **SNAKE AND SCORPION**
Envy's familiar companions
are the **snake (656)** and the
scorpion (657) – a symbolism
probably drawn from their venom,
which is equated with the poisonous tongue of an envious
or jealous person. (The scorpion can also appear, especially
in the Bible, as an emblem of hatred or treachery.)

The fabled **Lamia (658)** of Greek myth was a beautiful
snake-bodied woman who ate other people's children.
She was once a queen and was loved by Zeus, chief of the
Olympian deities, who was famous for his sexual exploits.
Out of revenge, his jealous wife, Hera, robbed Lamia of
her children, and turned her into a
demon. This terrifying tale symbolizes
the destructive chain of cause and
effect that jealousy can engender.

See also:

656 Protection, p.30
657 Health, p.80

659 BAT

European superstitions about
bats derived from the fact
that they are nocturnal
creatures who inhabit dark
places. In the Old Testament, the
bat is referred to as the "Devil's Bird".
Associations such as these led to an analogy between the
bat and the maliciousness of people who secretly spread
false rumours out of jealousy. Invidia, a medieval personification of Envy, has bat wings.

660–1 GREEN AND YELLOW

The greenish tinge of sickness led to the idea that people
sick with envy could turn **green (660)**. Shakespeare's Iago
tells Othello to "beware the green-eyed monster" of
jealousy, but is describing his own jealousy when he goes
on to say it "doth mock the meat it
feeds on". Iago is the green-eyed cat
who toys with Othello and feeds his
illusion that Desdemona is deceiving
him. **Yellow (661)** is the other hue
linked with envy, this time because it
is the colour of bile.

See also:

659 Fame and
Fortune, p.72; Evil,
pp.160–1

661 Defeat, Cowardice
and Betrayal, p.281

ANGER AND CRUELTY

662   ANGER PERSONIFIED
As with Envy, the personification of Anger turns the
emotion inwards – she is very often shown tearing apart her
own clothes. In medieval allegories of wrath, male figures
are sometimes depicted attacking monks and other defence-
less people. Two men duelling is another conventional way
to symbolize this vice.

663–4   STORMS AND VOLCANOES
Natural forces provided the most elemental
symbols of anger in the ancient world,
where violent **storms (663)** and thunder
were almost universally read as being
manifestations of divine wrath.
    The thunder gods made themselves
heard In Japan when their voices issued
forth from the **volcano (664)**. Female
deities were also feared in the Pacific
region, as in the Hawaiian legend
of the mother goddess Pele,
whose blazing and fearfully
unpredictable temper would
cause the Kilauea crater
to explode.

665 GIANTS

Fearful memories of parental or adult anger may account for the many stories of violent and cruel giants in mythology and literature. In general, giants symbolize brute force, uncontrolled rage and a degree of stupidity that enables heroes to overcome them, not by strength, but by intelligence. The biblical story of Goliath slain by David's slingshot is characteristic of the legends of many lands.

A race of one-eyed giants called the **Cyclops (666)** makes the symbolism of regressive anger still clearer. Odysseus encounters a Cyclops called Polyphemus, who greeted visitors by hurling rocks at them, and the hero has to outwit and blind him before he and his companions can escape.

667–8 LION AND TIGER

Both the **lion (667)** and **tiger (668)** can represent cruelty and anger, although they also have protective symbolism. Passages of the Bible use lion imagery to describe the wrath of God, suggesting a majestic, even righteous, quality of anger. However, the tiger, which is the third sign of the Chinese Zodiac, is one of the "Three Senseless Animals" in Chinese Buddhism and personifies Anger without any redeeming features.

See also:

667 Protection, p.29; Justice, p.181; Peace and Freedom, p.268

668 Protection, p.30

HAPPINESS AND JOY

669 BIRDS

In poetry and legend, nothing more frequently symbolizes joy than birds and their songs. Bleakness and melancholy are summed up by their absence, as in Keats' lines: "The sedge has withered from the lake/And no birds sing!" Some birds, such as the **magpie (670)**, an emblem in China of good luck, joy and sexual bliss, have negative symbolism elsewhere. But the range of positive associations is very wide –

See also:

674 Chastity and Virginity, p.201

unburdened liberty, freedom of movement, uplift, spontaneity, imagination, lightness of spirit and spirituality itself. At the level of folklore, small birds, such as the **wren (671)**, are

particularly linked with cheerfulness. The **bluebird (672)** was an emblem of happiness in the popular 1908 play of this name by the Symbolist writer Maeterlink.

673–4 COW AND ELEPHANT

Both the **cow (673)** and **elephant (674)** symbolize happiness in India and have had central roles in festive and ceremonial life for centuries. The lavishly decorated image of the playful elephant-headed Hindu god Ganesha is paraded through the streets of Bombay on his birthday.

675–6 PLUM AND NARCISSUS

The **plum (675)** is an emblem of marital happiness in China. Its positive symbolism there made it one of the "Three Friends of Winter", along with the pine and bamboo. Early-blooming plants are often emblems of joy and luck in China, and it is for this reason that the **narcissus (676)** is another Chinese symbol of a happy marriage.

677 MYRTLE

This fragrant evergreen shrub that grew wild in Mediterranean soils and was often used to make garlands or victor's wreaths was a Greek emblem of happiness, often used in marriage and childbirth rituals with this significance.

678 CLOUDS

Pink clouds represent happiness in Chinese art, a symbolism probably taken not only from the old farming lore that they presage good weather, but also from their association with the passage from an earthly state to a heavenly one. The idea that numinous clouds transport immortals on high is also found in some other cultures. In mystical thought, cloud nine represents the state of ultimate bliss.

679 ISLANDS

The belief that happiness lies somewhere else accounts for the many legends in which an enchanted island is a haven from worldly cares, griefs or disappointments. The Happy Isles of classical mythology and the Islands of the Blessed somewhere off the coasts of China, were heavens believed to be reserved for the elect. But in other tales, islands of happiness can be found by ordinary mortals, usually by voyaging westward. One of the attractions of islands such as the Celtic Tir na n'Og was the ability to recover one's youth. But, as in parallel Greek and Polynesian myths, men who find such islands often find themselves tiring of their delights.

GRIEF, MOURNING AND MELANCHOLIA

680 SATURN

Melancholia and pessimism are personified in planetary symbolism by Saturn. As a Roman god he was based on the Greek Cronus, said by Hesiod to have castrated his father with a scythe and later to have consumed his own children. Although Saturn was also an agricultural god with beneficent symbolism, medieval astrologers attached malign significance to the planet that bears his name and alchemists linked it with leaden darkness. Through a chain of misunderstandings, Saturn was conflated with Father Time in Western art. He is therefore shown as a greybeard with scythe and crutch, the companion of Death.

681–2 BLACK AND WHITE

Black (681) is conventionally the sign of mourning in Western tradition, and for this reason the gemstone most often associated with mourning is jet. As the expressions "black mood" and "black dog" show, black is also the indicator of despair and depression. In both cases, the implication is darkness without hope of a return to the light.

While wearing black is a symbolic manifestation of grief, its negativity is in contrast with older Christian traditions in which funerary clothes were **white (682)**, at least until the 4th century. Here, the symbolism was that death is a passage to a new life.

683 BLUE

The link between sadness and feeling "blue" is recent. The expression derives from folk songs sung at twilight by black American slaves and later developed into the music called the blues. The shadowy blue light of **twilight (684)** has more ancient associations with melancholia, especially in Northern Europe where its symbolism was used in Teutonic myths of the "Twilight of the Gods" – the Nordic Ragnarök and the German Götterdämmerung.

685 ASHES

Ashes symbolize the extinction of human life, even in cultures where burial, rather than cremation, is used to dispose of the dead. Ancient links between fire and the life-force underlie this symbolism, so that ashes are seen as the residue of both.

In both Arab and Hebrew custom, ashes were heaped upon the head as

See also:

682 Innocence, p.164; Purity and Incorruptibility p.216; Cowardice, pp.280–1; Divinity and Sanctity, p.306

a sign of mourning, and similar rituals are known from Egypt and Greece.

See also:

686–690
Fertility, p.53;
Beauty and Grace, p.132; Love, p.228; Peace and Freedom, p.267

686 Divinity and Sanctity, p.313

686 ROSE

Roses were scattered on Roman graves as funerary emblems of mourning to symbolize not only the painful brevity of human life but also the hope of life continuing in a world beyond this.

687 POPPY

The poppy was the attribute of the Greek gods Hypnos (sleep) and Morpheus (dreams), associations which made it also a symbol of the "winter sleep" of vegetation. Christianity later attached sacrificial meaning to the red poppy by drawing an analogy between its older symbolism and Christ's "sleep of death". It was against this background – as well as the poppied fields of Flanders – that the flower became a poignant symbol of remembrance for the fallen of the two world wars of the 20th century.

688 ANEMONE

In the rites of the Greek vegetation god Adonis, scarlet or crimson anemones were central emblems of grief, and loss.

According to Ovid's account of his death, Adonis was a beautiful youth loved by Venus, who could not dissuade him from hunting. When he was fatally gored by a boar, the sorrowing goddess sprinkled nectar on the bloodied ground where he lay and anemones sprang up to become his abiding memorial flowers.

689 IRIS

The sword-shaped leaves of the iris, particularly the gladiolus variety, were sometimes used in paintings of the Virgin Mary to suggest the sharp pain of Christ's Passion and also of Mary's grief.

690 ASPHODEL

This was the lily of the Elysian Fields in Greco-Roman mythology, perhaps because its grey leaves and pale yellow flowers suggested to Homer the diminished nature of the afterworld through which the dead moved like pale ghosts. It was often used as a funerary flower in the classical world.

See also:

690 Health (Plants), p.85

692 Purification, Atonement and Propitiation, pp.358–67

691 CYPRESS

The sombre appearance of the cypress, verging towards black as the tree ages, together with its rigid but dignified form, may have contributed to its choice as the preferred funerary tree of the early Mediterranean world, although as a resinous species it also had a positive link with incorruptibility. It was sacred to Hades and Pluto, and symbolizes mourning in Christian tradition.

692 RITUAL ACTIONS

Hundreds of different rituals have been used to manifest grief or underscore the importance of a death. Among the most common of such rituals in ancient societies were self-laceration, rending clothes, pulling out or cutting hair, various forms of abstinence and public displays of lamentation, sometimes provided by professional "mourners".

Stopping the clock (693), with its symbolism of silence, absence and finality, is one of many old European customs that are still observed in some areas.

INSTINCT, INTUITION
AND THE UNCONSCIOUS

694   ANIMALS

Widespread veneration of animal emblems in primitive cultures was often based on the belief that animals were superior to humans, not only in their physical and sensory abilities but also in their intuitive powers. Moving confidently through the night, they seemed in touch with the mysterious forces presumed to direct the course of human life. Later monotheistic religions tended to distrust instinct, intuition and the unconscious and to use animal symbols to depict these aspects of human nature negatively.

Carl Jung associated the dangerous aspects of the unconscious with the **bear (695)**. And the monstrous animal hybrids of mythology and legend are often explained by psychologists as dark projections of the human psyche, such as repressed fears, desires and aggressive urges.

696   FOREST

Jung linked the bear with psychic dangers because he saw the forest it inhabited as a primal symbol of the unconscious. This accounts, he thought, for the many European

See also:

696 Fertility, p.52

698 Fecundity and Plenty, p.57; Enlightenment and Transformation, p.343

folktales in which children are lost in the depths of a forest and have to overcome their own fears to find their way back to the light of day – a metaphor for acquiring the experience and self-knowledge to cope with adult life. As a place of moist, earthy, womb-like darkness, the forest is associated with the feminine principle and the intuitive powers of women.

697–8 LABYRINTH AND CAVE

The **labyrinth (697)** is another Jungian symbol of the unconscious, the journey through its maze standing for the perplexing process of self-discovery. This ties in with myths and rituals in which a **cave (698)** or grotto is a place of descent through

nightmarish tunnels of inquiry in search of knowledge or in the hope of re-emerging with a transfigured identity.

699 SEA

As a mysterious element, fluid, formless, unbounded and full of latent possibilities, the sea is a powerful symbol of the collective unconscious. The French interpreter of Greek

See also:

699 Fertility pp.49–50; Enlightenment and Transformation, p.342

mythology, Paul Diel, saw the violent god of the sea, Poseidon (Neptune), as a symbol of negative forces below the level of the conscious mind.

700 SHADOW

The shadow, equated with the soul in some primitive cultures, is a Jungian symbol of character faults, inconsistencies or destructive impulses at odds with a person's self-image but which nevertheless can have considerable subconscious influence. This "shadow" can appear in dreams as an adversary figure. Symbolic inversion of this kind was sometimes represented in ancient cultures by the **dwarf (701)**, who might play the fool to a king. Gnomes and other dwarfish creatures often have adversarial roles in legends and are widely connected with shadowy caves, the underworld, instinct and intuitive knowledge.

702 MOON

Presiding as it does over night, sleep and dreams, the moon is associated with intuition, subjectivity and the revelation or release of unconscious wishes. It is, of course, a major feminine symbol, and women are themselves symbolically linked with intuition and the unconscious.

States and Conditions

Peace and Freedom 266

War and Victory 272

Defeat, Cowardice and
Betrayal 280

Duality and Union 282

Harmony and Meditation . . . 290

Death 294

PEACE AND FREEDOM

703–6   DOVE AND OLIVE

The **dove (703)** is an example of a visual symbol perfectly fitting the concept it represents. Its rounded head, small bill, plump, white body and throaty murmuring have made it a universally recognized emblem not only of peace but also of pacifism. In Western art, the figure of Peace has a dove and **olive (704)** branch as attributes – a reference to the biblical story of Noah releasing from the Ark first a black raven, then a white dove, to find out if the Flood had abated and there was any sign of life. The dove brought back an olive leaf in its beak, representing a pledge of peace between God and humans.

Another sign of this pact was the **rainbow (705)**. "I have set my bow in the clouds, and it shall be a sign of the covenant between me and the earth", God says in Genesis.

The olive itself has another, separate, association with peace because the Romans used it as an emblem of the *Pax Romana*. Envoys of rebellious provinces or hostile powers brought an olive branch to symbolize their submission to imperial authority. Another peace emblem used by Rome, and Greece before it, was **laurel (706)**.

See also:

704 Fecundity and Plenty, p.62; Chastity and Virginity, p.201

705 Wealth and Prosperity, p.67;

707 Grief, Mourning and Melancholia pp.257–8

707 FLOWERS

Flowers have been given as emblems of reconciliation for centuries. But in the 1960s, this association was poetically extended when the "flower power" generation used flowers as emblems of universal love and peace. This symbolism, captured in photographs of anti-war protesters poking flowers into soldiers' gun barrels, played a significant part in mobilizing American opposition to the Vietnam war.

708 ISLANDS

Because they were often refuges from storms, islands appear in mythology and religion as places of tranquillity. For Hindus, the legendary Island of the Blessed is an emblem of spiritual peace in the agitation of material existence.

709 NIGHT

Night is a highly ambivalent symbol, but peace and refuge from care are among its positive emblematic meanings. In art its Greek personification, the goddess Nyx, is shown as the winged mother of two children, a white one representing sleep, a dark one representing death. Sleep was personified in Greek mythology by a youthful god, **Hypnos (710)**, who sometimes appears in art wearing a poppy in his hair, symbolizing the narcotic-like tranquillity of deep sleep.

711–2 LION AND LAMB

Images of a **lion (711)** and **lamb (712)** – emblems of fierceness and gentleness – lying companionably together symbolize peace in both Christian and Mughal art. The concept of a "peaceable kingdom", in which nature is not red in tooth and claw, remains a popular theme of Naïve painting.

713 SADDLE

In China, phonetic associations between "saddle" and "peace" made the saddle a symbol of harmonious domestic life. It was an ancient custom for a bride to step over a saddle at the entrance to the parental home of her husband.

714 PEACE PIPE

The calumet of Native North Americans acquired the name peace pipe because it was ceremonially smoked to symbolize the good faith of both parties to a peace accord. More generally, the pipe was offered as a symbol of hospitality. As it was sometimes smoked to cement treaties of war, it was a more ambiguous symbol than its popular name suggests. The smoke itself was seen as a means of communicating with higher powers whose help would be needed in either contingency.

715   CORNUCOPIA

The cornucopia is often an attribute in art of the winged figure of Peace. The symbolism here is that prosperity and agricultural abundance are only possible if war is laid aside.

See also:

711 Anger and Cruelty, p.248

716   BROKEN WEAPONS

The figure of Peace in art is sometimes shown with broken weapons or weapons thrown on a bonfire. The same symbolism appears in Native North American traditions, where bundled or broken arrows signified peace.

717 FREEDOM PERSONIFIED

The most famous symbol of freedom is Frédéric-Auguste Bartholdi's towering Statue of Liberty, presented to the American people by France to mark the centenary of the American Declaration of Independence and the friendship between the two countries. The **flaming torch (718)** held by the figure of Liberty is itself an emblem of freedom. In art, it is the attribute of Prometheus, who seized fire from the gods – a symbol of the human struggle for autonomy.

719 PHRYGIAN CAP

This conical bonnet with a furled front originated in Persia, was adopted as the headwear of freemen in the Phrygian region of Asia Minor, and was subsequently given by the Romans to freed slaves as an emblem of their new status.

See also:

720 Strength and Stability, p.113

It was taken up as a symbol of liberty during the French Revolution and is worn by the gun-carrying, bare-breasted figure of Liberty in Delacroix's stirring picture *Liberty Leading the People* (opposite), celebrating a later revolution in 1830.

720 LONG HAIR

Long hair was worn by warriors of many tribes on the fringes of the Roman Empire as a symbol of freedom or independence, especially by the Gauls and other Celtic people. The same symbolism was taken up in the hippie culture of the 1960s.

WAR AND VICTORY

721 MARS

Mars is the best known personification of war in Western art and literature. Based on the Greek god Ares, he changed from an Italian agricultural god to a god of war as Rome expanded its empire by force. Returning conquerors made sacrifices to him, and Roman soldiers drilled and honed their military skills on the "Field of Mars". Mars was on the losing

side to his female counterpart, Minerva (Athene), in legends of the Trojan War. Renaissance painters, such as Botticelli, often show him unmanned by his love for Venus (see below).

722 FLAG

Although flags now represent many things other than war, military dominance was often the symbolism of the earliest

known standards used in Egypt, Persia and other parts of the ancient world. These bore personal emblems of individual rulers or of aggressive animals with totemic significance, such as the wolf. Supremacy was implied by the height of the standard itself. Flags, banners and pennants also had practical value as identification insignia in the confusion of battle, but their assertive symbolism is shown by the importance attached to their loss or capture. The tricolour of the French revolution and the red flag of socialism are examples of the way in which flags can transcend national boundaries as militant rallying symbols.

723 WAR DANCE

Ancient war dances sometimes had ritual symbolism in addition to their usefulness in unifying and stirring the blood of a fighting force. By enacting both attack and defence, the dance symbolized the battle itself, seeking to ensure victory through a form of sympathetic magic. Survivals of this tradition can be seen in the sword dances of the Scots and Pathans.

724 PREDATORS

As the modern idiom of the political **hawk (725)** shows, predatory birds are often emblems of war or victory. Both the **raven (726)** and **crow (727)** have positive symbolism elsewhere, but in European tradition, as companions of

See also:

723 Duality and Union, p.288; Death, p.296

727 Bad Luck, p.78

729 Faith and Hope, p.179

war gods such as the Teutonic Wodan, were associated with battles and death.

The major animal symbol of military supremacy is the **eagle (728)**. From the time of the founding of the Roman Republic, this was the emblem carried on its standards as the bird of its supreme god, Jupiter. The Hittites used a double-headed eagle device which later became the battle emblem of the Seljuk Turks and the imperial emblem of both the Holy Roman Empire and the Russian Empire. Napoleon deployed massed eagle standards to symbolize the military victories of his own self-made empire, a triumphal device also used by the Nazis in their annual Nuremberg rallies. The eagle's symbolism of victory is shared by another master of the skies, the **falcon (729)**

730 VICTORY PERSONIFIED

The Greek deity Nike is the winged figure used in Western art to symbolize victory. Called "war champion", she was hymned as the daughter of the mighty god of war, Ares (Mars), but she also had an important emblematic role in the ancient Olympic Games which were held in honour of the gods. Zeus was depicted in his sanctuary at Olympia holding Nike in his right hand.

In 1811, the sculptor Canova completed a colossal nude statue of Napoleon carrying a globe on which Nike stood with arms upraised. The symbolic wheel turned full circle when this statue was presented to Wellington to celebrate his victory at Waterloo. Prophetically, Napoleon had disliked the statue, partly because Nike was positioned so that she turned away from him.

731 TRIUMPHAL ARCH

The triumphal arch with narrative carvings of victorious scenes is one of the most characteristic of all Roman monuments. The arch already had symbolic links with supremacy in the Greco-Roman world by analogy with the overarching sky, an emblem of Jupiter. The Arc de Triomphe in Paris was built to celebrate Napoleon's successive victories over Austria, Prussia and Russia in 1805–8.

732 ANIMALS

Several animals symbolize victory, notably the **lion (733)** and **horse (734)**, emblems of spiritual as well as military victory. Christ is sometimes shown riding a white horse as a conquering spirit. The Romans superstitiously believed that victory would be theirs if their advancing troops sighted a **wolf (735)** before battle – a probable reference to the wolf's legendary association with the military hero of Rome's founding, Romulus.

Victory over death is sometimes personified

See also:

735 Femininity and Maternity, p.126; Evil, p.162

by the legendary **phoenix (736)**, which has this meaning in early Christian funerary sculpture. On Roman coins, it symbolized Rome's boast that it would always survive military setbacks and rise again victorious.

737   FIVE-POINTED STAR

The five-pointed star, an ancient emblem of the Assyrian warrior goddess Ishtar (a divine personification of the planet Venus), became a more widespread symbol of both military and spiritual ascendancy, notably as the star with the crescent on the Islamic flag. It is the star most often used in military and police insignia, usually with one point up and two down – its positive aspect in traditional symbolism.

738   PALM FRONDS

Palm trees, with their solar-like spread of strong leaves, were venerated in the ancient world, and the custom of awarding victors with palm fronds is based on their stature and evergreen habit. Branches were carried as triumphal emblems in Roman processions, and given to victorious gladiators. The figure of Victory often holds a palm frond in Western art. Christianity took over and spiritualized this symbolism following the apostle John's account of people strewing palm leaves before Jesus as he entered Jerusalem on what is now known as Palm Sunday. Symbolizing victory over death, the palm became the attribute of many Christian saints. Pilgrims to the Holy Land were called "palmers", from their custom of bringing a palm frond back to their home church.

See also:

737 Protection, p.20; Harmony and Meditation, p.290

738 Death, p.295

739 LAUREL WREATH

The Greeks used the aromatic bay species of laurel as a living crown for victorious athletes, poets and musicians at the Pythian games, dedicated to Apollo. The god was said to have used this plant to purify himself in the groves of Tempe in Thessaly after he had slain the serpent-monster Python with a thousand arrows. The fame of his cult at Delphi meant that the laurel eventually displaced wreaths of olive, parsley and pine which had the same symbolism but were associated with other gods.

DEFEAT, COWARDICE AND BETRAYAL

740 YOKE

The yoke appears in the Bible as an emblem of submission and was well known in the Roman world as a symbolic means of humiliating defeated armies. Beaten troops were forced to pile their weapons and walk under a yoke-shaped structure to acknowledge their submission – a ritual famously turned against the Romans when one of their own armies was captured at Caudine Forks by the Samnites, their strongest Italian adversaries in the 4th century BCE.

The yoke aso symbolizes slavery – often the fate of defeated enemies. Arab slave traders used yokes to transport people to market. In Christian symbolism the yoke has more positive meaning, signifying obedient submission to religious vows, a burden freely taken up.

741 WHITE

Perhaps because skin pallor was thought to be a sign of cowardice, white has for centuries been the colour of surrender. The **white flag (742)** is a universally understood symbol of non-resistance or of an appeal for a cease-fire. The use of a **white feather (743)** as an emblem of cowardice derives from cockfighting. Beaten gamecocks showed white feathers when they lifted their hackles to signal that they had had enough. Accusatory white feathers were sent to men thought to be avoiding military service in World War I.

744 YELLOW

Yellow became an English synonym for fear or cowardice not only because it was linked with skin pallor but also because pale yellow was traditionally feared as an emblem of disease. Yellow crosses were painted on houses afflicted by the plague in London during the 17th century, and quarantine was indicated by yellow flags.

Yellow is also symbolically linked with treachery – one of its code meanings in traditional Chinese theatre. The belief that the Jews had "betrayed" Jesus led the Christian Church in medieval Europe to prescribe that Jews should wear yellow badges, an idea taken up with still more sinister motives in Nazi Germany, where yellow stars were stiched onto their clothes. Judas Iscariot is sometimes shown wearing yellow in Christian art.

See also:

741 Innocence, p.164; Purity and Incorruptibility, p.216; Divinity and Sanctity, p.306

DUALITY AND UNION

745 YIN-YANG (TAIJI TU) SYMBOL

The Chinese yin-yang symbol known as the Taiji Tu or "diagram of the supreme ultimate" may have been created as long as 1,200 years ago, and no graphic symbol captures a philosophical idea more simply. It represents duality as the dynamic force in the cosmos. Curled together to form a circle are two fish-like shapes, one bright, one dark, each containing a smaller circle of the opposite colour. This gives the image spiralling fluidity and at the same time perfect balance. The whole sums up the Taoist "Way" – the acceptance that all things are the product of two constantly interacting forces that are contrary but necessary to each other.

The yin (dark, passive, feminine) and yang (light, active, masculine) elements of the symbol are interpreted by Taoist and Buddhist teachers in a great variety of ways – shadow/sun, earth/heaven, moisture/dryness, intuition/reason, obscurity/illumination, non-being/being.

The **I Ching (746)**, or predictive *Book of Changes*, is based on a similar interplay of opposite forces, shown as patterns of continuous (yin) or broken (yang) lines. These appear together with the Taiji Tu symbol on the flag of South Korea.

747 TWINS

Twins can symbolize either cooperative dualism or disunity.
In Greek mythology, the twins of the Gemini constellation,
Castor and Polydeuces (called Pollux by the Romans),
cooperate to protect seafarers by calming storms. The story
that Zeus fathered one of the twins ties in with ancient
superstitions that the birth of twins must involve some
kind of supernatural agency.

The mother of Romulus and Remus, who was a Vestal
Virgin, explained their birth by saying their father was Mars.
The twins quarrelled and Romulus slew his brother. Similar
conflicts appear in Native North American legends, where
one twin symbolizes good and the other evil. In some early
societies, twins were thought to be bad omens and were
killed at birth.

748 DOUBLES

The doubling of an image is often a means of heightening
its symbolic power. But human doubles have usually had
negative symbolism, suggesting duplicity, stolen identity,
the existence of a dangerous second nature or even demonic
possession. These themes have all been explored in literature,
the German doppelgänger appearing as a ghostly figure,
sometimes symbolizing retribution.

749 ANKH

The ankh, an ancient Egyptian symbol for "life", is a geometric sign in the form of a T cross surmounted by an oval loop, often held by the goddess Isis or other gods, but also by pharaohs. Among the many explanations of its significance is that it represents the union or reconciliation of opposites, particularly of male and female principles, expressed in the form of a key to life as well as death.

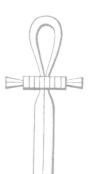

750 HEXAGRAM

The hexagram, which is formed by two overlapping triangles, one upright, the other inverted, is an ancient symbol of synthesis or of unity in duality. Alchemists used it as a sign for the dual power of fire (masculine) and water (feminine). More famously, it is now the emblem of Israel as the Star of David, so called because it was King David who unified the formerly warring states of Judah and Israel. The number **six (751)** is itself a symbol of union, possibly due to the fact that it was widely linked with balance and stability.

752 TRIANGLE

Other triangular forms can also symbolize the union of
opposing principles, as in the sexual sign of male and female
triangles meeting at their points. Positioned with their bases
meeting, two triangles represent the waxing and waning
phases of the moon.

753 DRAGON DISK

Although normally a solar emblem, the frequently seen
Chinese images of a disk encircled by clawed dragons
contending with each other symbolizes the reconciliation of
opposing forces. Alternatively, the combatants may be snakes.

54–5 SQUARE AND CIRCLE

In the many Hindu mandalas based on a **square (754)** within
a **circle (755)**, the symbolism is the union of earth and heav-
en, the square being a widely recognized sign for the earth,
the circle representing the celestial sphere. This is the emblematic meaning of domed temples built on a square plan.

56–7 CHAIN AND NECKLACE

The joined links of a **chain (756)** have been a symbol of
union since antiquity. Homer himself wrote of a golden chain
hung in the heavens by Zeus and linking the celestial and

earthly spheres. The decorative chains at weddings, reunions and festivities celebrate social or family cohesion. A **necklace (757)** can also be used as an emblem of union or of unity in diversity. In Polynesian custom, the garland of flowers called the lei symbolically links hosts and guests.

758 MARRIAGE

In ancient societies, marriage was one of life's most significant rites of passage, an affirmation of continuing order on

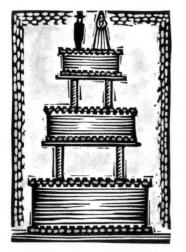

both the human and cosmic scale. It symbolized a binding union between two opposite principles, male and female, seen as necessary to create and protect new life. In myth and art, key dualities – god and goddess, king and queen, sun and moon, heaven and earth, the sulphur and mercury of alchemists – appear constantly as emblems of wholeness and guarantees against chaos.

Among the unifying symbols still used at weddings are

the **ring (759)**, emblem of the indivisible and eternal; the **joining of hands (760)**; the **wedding cake (761)**, unifying two families in shared food; and, in India, the **knot (762)**, which the Hindu bridegroom ties in a ribbon around the neck of the bride.

763 CIRCLE

The linked rings shown on the Olympic flag draw on the unifying symbolism of the circle as a geometric form implying inclusiveness. The **Round Table (764)** of Arthurian legend has similar meaning: Arthur's knights, bound together by their vow of loyalty, were part of an élite democratic circle, of which the round table was a symbol. However, inclusiveness within a circle suggests exclusion outside it. This is evident in modern idiom.

To join someone's "circle" of friends is to be admitted to a unified but privileged group of people.

See also:

759 Protection, p.20

762 Protection, p.23

765 DOUBLE SPIRAL

Double spiral motifs symbolize unity in duality. An early example is the **caduceus (766)**, the Greco-Roman herald's staff, on which two spiralling snakes form an image of opposing forces unified. In Celtic art, the sinuous, interlaced forms decorating hundreds of ancient images suggest not only delight in intricate patterning but also an awareness of the creative tension inherent in the cosmos. The discovery that the human genetic code is carried on an interweaving spiral called the double helix further reflects the ubiquity of the spiral in nature and in living organisms.

767 DANCE

Union was the symbolism of many ancient dance forms. This is still true of linked dancing to set patterns (as in folk dances), or of dances that allow group expression of joy as at weddings. But more primitive dances symbolized union with cosmic forces, the setting up of an energy field that could link the dancers with the supernatural realm and draw down support, protection, fertility or healing powers. The wild dancing of orgiastic religious cults represented an effort to transcend the human state and merge with the divine.

768–9 BLOOD AND BREAD

The mingling of **blood (768)** is an age-old means of symbolizing a close and lasting union between friends or lovers. The emblematic power of a blood brotherhood is the ancient belief that blood is the living spirit of a person and that an exchange of blood establishes a spiritual bond between people, whether it is done by ritual slashing or by a mere pin-prick.

The breaking and sharing of **bread (769)** is also a symbol of union that reaches far back in history. Blood, drunk in the symbolic form of wine, and bread, eaten in the symbolic form of a wafer, are the key elements of the Christian Eucharist, which draws on these older traditions in order to suggest spiritual union with a redeeming saviour.

See also:

766 Protection, p.30

767 War and Victory, p.274; Death, p.296

HARMONY AND MEDITATION

770–1 PENTAGRAM AND FIVE

The **pentagram (770)**, a five-pointed geometric form, was regarded by the Greek philosopher and number theorist Pythagoras as a symbol of mystic harmony. He and his followers referred to it as Hugieia, which is often translated as "health" but whose sense is better understood as "wholeness". For him, the significance of the emblem was that its **five (771)** points were the sum of the numbers two (which he took to be feminine and terrestial) and three (masculine and celestial). Thus, the number five symbolized the cosmic harmony of opposites, the marriage of heaven and earth.

772 MUSIC

In China, musical harmonies were symbols of how disparate things could be reconciled by the vital force of duality. The semitones of the earliest Chinese octave were thus assigned ying or yang qualities. The symbolism of music and numbers was closely linked in both China and Greece, and thought to be the key to planetary relationships. Plato thought the whole universe formed a musical scale and number, and made an analogy between the relative speeds at which planets moved and the changing vibrations of different strings on a lyre.

See also:

770 War and Victory, p.278

773 Fecundity and Plenty p.57

773 GARDEN

The biblical description of the Eden from which Adam and Eve were expelled led to an emblematic link between the garden and a divinely ordered world. However, this is not simply a Judeo-Christian concept. In most cultures, and particularly in Japan, the creation of a perfectly balanced garden has been taken to symbolize the ability of humans themselves to achieve a state of spiritual harmony.

774 MANDALA

The carefully balanced patterns of ancient Hindu and Buddhist mandalas symbolize a divine harmony underlying the disordered chaos of the material world. Within an outer (terrestial) square, concentric elements of the design enclose a sacred space which an adept may enter by focusing on the whole image until it is internally visualized. Progression towards the centre is then achieved by meditating until individual consciousness dissolves into cosmic consciousness.

For Jung, the mandala was a symbol of the human psyche, progression to the centre being analogous to discovery of the self, resulting in a balanced view of life.

The **yantra (775)**, or "instrument", particularly associated with Tantric Buddhism, is a more spare, linear symbol of the cosmos. In meditation, its triangles and other geometric shapes are used to build up a mental picture of force lines leading to the bindu or point of creation itself, from which everything expands and to which everything returns.

776 TEA

Tranquillity and harmony are symbolized by the purist etiquette of the Zen Buddhist tea ceremony. According to Japanese legend, the Bodhidharma meditated with such intensity that he cut off his own eyelids to prevent himself breaking his trance by falling asleep. From the fallen eyelids grew the first tea plants.

777 BREATHING

The symbolic importance of controlled breathing in Muslim, Hindu and Buddhist meditation is that it is thought to concentrate the spirit. In its most advanced form, Hindu yogis believe that they can align themselves with the rhythmic flow of the universe itself.

DEATH

778 DEATH PERSONIFIED

The notion of Death as a figure who can enter the earthly world to claim a victim has long been a popular theme in literature, theatre and film because it suggests the possibility of outfighting or outwitting a divinity who has unwisely taken on material form.

The Greek personification of Death was a pitiless, dark-cloaked god called **Thanatos (779)**, mythical son of Night and brother of Sleep. In Euripides' play Alcestis, Herakles wrestles with him and forces him to release Alcestis who has offered her life in exchange for her husband's.

In art, the symbolism is more uncompromising. Death is a **skeleton (780)**, often hooded and carrying a scythe, sickle or sword. He may hold an hour-glass, symbolizing that someone's time is up. As a mounted figure reaping bodies like a whirlwind, he symbolizes death on the wider scale of pestilence or war. The devastating outbreaks of the plague that took place in 14th-century Europe made the skeleton an omnipresent symbol of mortality and led to a whole series of different paintings on the theme of "The Triumph of Death".

More gentle personifications of Death are a veiled or winged woman, often seen on war graves with her hand resting on the shoulder of a soldier.

In many myths and legends, heralds of death, such as the Breton **Ankou (781)**, whose head is shaded with a broad hat, serve gods of the underworld who rule over the dead but dispatch auxiliaries to bring souls to them. The Islamic harbinger of death is the angel **Izrael (782)**.

783 PALM

In Christian art, a palm frond is sometimes a symbol of approaching death. In a reprise of the Annunciation, the archangel Michael is shown bringing one to the Virgin Mary just before her death. The meaning of this is that the "palm" of paradise awaits her, that death is only a passage to spiritual life.

See also:

779 Peace and Freedom (Night), p.267

783 War and Victory, p.278

784–5   OIL AND FASTING

Ritual symbolism surrounding death is common before as well as after the event, when the end of life is seen as the dissolution of the body but not the soul. In the Roman Catholic sacrament of Extreme Unction, a priest anoints the senses (hearing, sight, smell, taste, touch) and the feet of the dying with consecrated **oil (784)** to symbolize the remission of sins through Christ.

In religions without a saving intermediary, preparation for death is seen as an individual responsibility. Jain ascetics have been known to engage in **fasting (785)** to death as a symbolic means of purging the body of negative karma and progressing to a higher level of spiritual awareness.

786   DANCE

Death appears as a dancer, or sometimes as a **drummer (787)** in many cultures, sometimes waltzing with the Devil or with a young woman – to make the point that the young and beautiful are as vulnerable as the old and ugly. The concept of death as the great leveller was symbolized in medieval Western art and drama by the **danse macabre (788)** in which skeletons partner representatives of all classes of society, from pope to lowly serf. In medieval

See also:

786 Protection Procession), p.21;
War and Victory, p.274;
Duality and Union, p.288

superstition, skeletons were believed to rise from graves and perform a **Dance of Death (789)** in the dead of night.

Death can appear as a seductive female dancer in Hindu art. More powerful images of **Shiva (790)**, ringed by fire as Lord of Death as well as Dance, symbolize the Vedic idea

that death must be seen as part of the creative process that animates the universe.

791–4 VOYAGES AND DEATH SHIPS

Death is often envisaged as the beginning of a **voyage** (791). Apart from the spectacular funerary ships provided by the Vikings, who burnt their chieftains on longships, many societies have cast bodies adrift on simple boats – in effect, **death ships (792)** – seen as symbolic cradles for those about to be reborn. In Egypt, the blessed dead could

hope to join the sun god on his nightly voyage by barque through the underworld. The discovery of cedar boats beside the tombs of dignitaries shows the power of this symbolism.

So persuasive was the classical myth of the ferryman, Charon, whose boat carried souls to the underworld, that it was customary in ancient Greece to bury the dead with a **coin (793)** in the mouth to pay him. The idea that the soul is a voyager underlies the ancient belief among coastal peoples that a dying man will take his last breath on an **ebb tide (794)**.

795 ANIMALS

Animals associated with death range from winged creatures, such as the owl, crow, raven and bat, all with somewhat sinister symbolism, to psychopomps (soul-guides), such as the **dog (796)**, which appears in many different cultures as a companion in the transition from life to death. Jackals, like the Egyptian **Anubis (797)**, who led souls to justice, and **wolves (798)** in North American Indian legends, share this symbolism.

In ancient Parsee custom, a dog was brought to deathbeds so that the dying person could see the afterworld in the reflective surface of its eyes. In the Americas, the Aztec dog-god Xoltl

See also:
798 Evil, p.162

had a protective role in the underworld, and a dog-god carried souls across the Mayan river of death. The **dolphin (799)** played a similar role in Cretan, Etruscan and Greek legends by carrying souls to the Islands of the Blessed.

The **horse (800)** is another animal emblematically associated with death and with passage to the afterworld. Images of horses have been found on the walls of some underground burial chambers, probably with this significance. Like the dog, the horse's keen sensory perception led to the belief that it was in touch with the spirit world, and this may be the basis of the old custom of leading a **riderless horse (801)** at military or state funerals. Superstitions and legends often suggest that horses can see spirits of the dead or be ridden

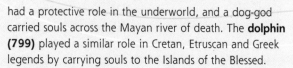

by them, as in ghost stories of a **headless horseman (802)**. By association with the pallor of death, such ghostly horses are usually pale, as is the horse ridden by Death in the Book of Revelation.

See also:

799 Salvation and Redemption, p.318

803 Protection, p.26

803 BELL

The bell is a symbol of the divine voice, and it was formerly rung not only to announce a death or funeral, but also just before a death, when it was called the **passing bell (804)**. The intention of this custom was to ensure that a dying

person's soul could pass safely to the other world because
evil spirits would keep their distance while the bell rang.

805 COMET

Comets, like other unusual cosmic events, traditionally
had ominous symbolism and were once thought to presage
the death of great men. "When beggars die, there are no
comets seen/The heavens themselves blaze forth the death
of princes", wrote Shakespeare in Julius Caesar.

Spiritual Life

Divinity and Sanctity 304

Salvation and Redemption . . . 316

Images of the Soul 322

Immortality and Eternity 325

Rebirth and Resurrection . . . 330

Enlightenment
and Transformation 340

Ascension and
Axial Interchange 348

Purification, Atonement
and Propitiation 358

Divination 368

DIVINITY AND SANCTITY

806 LIGHT

In many religions, light and divinity are almost synonymous, as can be seen by the epithets often substituted for the name of a sacred figure. Allah is called the Light of Heaven and Earth; Christ the Light of the World and Gautama Buddha the Light of Asia. More ancient sun and fire cults lie behind the symbolism of the various forms of **nimbus (807)** or emanation of light used by artists to indicate the divinity or sanctity of a figure. Apollo in the Greek world and Mithras in the Middle East are among sun gods who were shown with radiating lines or beams around their heads, later called the **corona (808)** or Crown of Gold. The nimbus around the head of Christ can sometimes appear in the form of the **Cross of Light (809)**.

Artists of the late 16th century, such as Titian, often used light flooding the background of a painting to symbolize divinity. The spiritual symbolism of light was also the driving force of the architectural revolution which produced Gothic cathedrals. The object of their great curtain walls of **stained glass (810)** was to "render immaterial all that is material".

811 HALO

This circular form of radiance became common in Byzantine art of the 6th century, used to symbolize not only

See also:

806 Knowledge and Learning, p.134; Grief, Mourning and Melancholia (Twilight), p.255

the divinity of Christ but also the sanctity of the Holy Family, angels, saints and even the Emperor and his wife as God's representatives on earth. It was usually painted as a flat disc behind the head, although a halo in the form of a floating ring was introduced to church art during the Renaissance and survives as a satirical emblem of virtue today.

812 GOLD

The symbolism of light, sun and fire – and therefore of divinity – combine in the metal and the tincture it lends its name to. In sacred art, the use of **gilding (813)** by Byzantine artists and, later, by Russian icon makers and many medieval European artists, was intended to symbolize divine radiance as well as to catch the light in churches. Gold is also a sacred hue in Buddhism. In Egypt, the metal itself was identified as the flesh of the sun-god Ra, and in Mexico as the faeces of Huitzilopochtli, the Atzec god of the sun.

814 WHITE

Because it is the colour of maximum light, white is the symbol of spirituality and sanctity as well as of purity. It has been worn by priestly orders in many civilizations as well as in the Christian world, most notably by the Pope.

815 SUN

The sun was seen everywhere as the centre of the universe and has been worshipped as an actual divinity in innumerable cultures and traditions, if not always as the supreme deity. The Emperors of Rome abandoned the cult of Sol, their sun deity, only when Constantine converted to Christianity in 324CE. So popular with the Roman army was the male solar cult of Mithraism (based on the Indo-Iranian sun god) in the 3rd century, that the Emperor Aurelian named 25 December as the birthday of Mithras, the "Unconquerable Sun" – a choice of date which was soon taken over by Christianity as the emblematic birthday of Jesus, the new God of Light.

In Peru and Egypt, where sun cults reached their highest form of development, the supposed kinship between the monarchy and the "father" god, allowed kings to claim divine status for themselves.

Purely as a symbol of divinity, the sun is often seen as the principle agent of a supreme being. In Christian, Islamic and Hindu tradition, it represents the **Eye of God (816)**, an embodiment of his all-knowing, all-seeing power and a guiding force radiating love and life-force. Dante declared that no other visible thing was a more suitable symbol of God himself.

See also:

812 Wealth and Prosperity, p.66

814 Grief, Mourning and Melancholia, p.255; Defeat, Cowardice and Betrayal, p.280

817 DISK

The disk is the most common emblem of the divine sun in Egypt and and throughout the Middle East. It also appears in the form of a rayed disk in India, associated particularly with the power of Vishnu.

By symbolic extension the winged disk, incorporating the emblematic supremacy of the eagle, can stand for both sun and sky gods. It was the sign of the Iranian god of light, Ahura Mazda, and of Shamash and Asshur in Babylonia and Assyria.

818 MOON

In most early cultures, the moon was a divinity second only to the sun; in a few, it was the father god himself, notably in Japan, Oceania and the ancient Teutonic world. But apart from the association between the crescent moon and the Virgin Mary, the moon seldom appears purely as a symbol of the state of divinity

819 FIRE

In ancient Iran, fire was revered as a manifestation of divinity and was thought to provide its central dwelling place. The same symbolism appears in North American Indian traditions. Fire is also a symbol in the Bible for the presence of

See also:

818 Femininity and
Maternity p.123

819 Ascension and
Axial Interchange,
p.341; Purification,
Atonement and
Propitiation, p.359

Yahweh, who speaks from a burning
mountain, a burning bush and a pillar of fire
(also an emblem used for the Buddha).

The **flame (820)** is an emblem of divinity
in Chinese art, and represents the divine spirit
when it is shown within a triangle in alchemical illustrations. It is an attribute of the
Indian gods Vishnu, Shiva and Krishna. In
Christianity, a lamp or candle burning in a
niche symbolizes the presence of divinity.

821 PLANETS

For thousands of years, planets were believed to be living
divinities and were personified by gods and goddesses
whose characteristics and powers were popularly known
through the symbol systems of mythology. In addition to
the sun and moon, then classed as planets, five other visible
heavenly bodies were thought to influence the course of
human life. These are now known by the Roman names of
the divinities who personified them. In order of status they
were: **Jupiter (822)**, called Zeus in Greece and Marduk in
Mesopotamia; **Saturn (823)**, Cronos, Ninib; **Mercury
(824)**, Hermes, Nabu; **Venus (825)**, Aphrodite, Ishtar;
and **Mars (826)**, Ares, Nergal.

The divinities representing planets in art are often shown with a **star (827)**, another symbol of divinity. A **four-pointed star (828)** was a sign used for the Babylonian sun god Shamash. Many Queens of Heaven wear a **Crown of Stars (829)**, including Ishtar in Mesopotamia, Isis in Egypt and the Virgin Mary.

830 SUPREME BEING

Early belief in a supreme being was widespread, and not confined simply to monotheistic traditions. But symbols representing this higher form of divinity are remarkably few. This may reflect a general feeling that such a being (or "non-being") cannot be known, visualized or even named. Although the Bible talks of "God", or the "Lord", his sacred name in Hebrew is simply the four letters YHWH, "Yahweh". Some have translated this as "I am".

In Christian art, the figure of God as a venerable **Father (831)** with long beard and locks begins to appear only in the Renaissance (based probably on classical images of Jupiter). Before this time, Jesus alone was shown as God incarnated.

The number **One (832)** is a symbol for God in Judeo-Christian tradition and also in Islam, where images of Allah are forbidden as blasphemous. Other Christian emblems

include a **hand (833)** stretching out from a cloud, an
eye (834), or an eye in
a triangle. The **trian-
gle (835)** represents
the Christian Trinity
– God the Father,
God the Son and
God the Holy Spirit –
the symbol of an indi-
visible divinity revealing
itself in different forms.
Sometimes, God is shown with
a **triangular halo (836)**. The Trinity is also
symbolized by three entwined **fish (837)** or a fish with
three heads. This derives from the use of the fish as an
early Christian symbol for Christ, which has been found
on seals and lamps in Rome. Other religions have attached
sacramental meaning to the fish, but it became a secret
emblem for Jesus because the Greek word for
fish could form an acronym for "Jesus Christ,
Son of God, Saviour". In figurative art, the Trinity
is shown as God and Christ with a **dove (838)**
representing the Holy Spirit.

See also:

837 Fertility,
p.49; Wealth and
Prosperity, p.66

839 TRIMURTI

Brahma, Vishnu and Shiva symbolize a divine unity in Indian art, often shown as a three-headed figure called the Trimurti. This sacred triad does not imply a monotheistic being such as the Christian Trinity but is a condensed image of the cycles of creation, preservation and destruction in the material universe. Shiva alone can appear as a triad with this meaning. His triple powers are also represented by a **trident (840)**, a symbol sometimes used as a forehead mark by his cult followers.

841 CENTRE

The centre is a symbol of pure being in all major religions, the essence of the godhead or the dwelling place of divinity.

In metaphysics, it is represented as a **point (842)** which concentrates and contains the meaning of everything else. Axial symbols of all kinds, ranging from pillars to mountains or stepped temples, can represent the centre. In graphic form it is sometimes shown as a dot or small circle within a cross form, or as a dot or small cross within a circle. The dot in a circle is also an ancient sign of sun gods.

The emblem of the Cabbalistic society of Rosicrucians showed a **rose (843)** at the centre of a cross, symbolizing the heart of Christ, the divine light at the centre of the wheel of life.

844 SWASTIKA

To the ancients, the swastika suggested the four directions of space and the solar momentum of a turning wheel with light streaming back from its spokes. It was a sign of sun and sky gods in the ancient world, particularly in Indo-Iranian cults. (This is the basis for its use by anti-Semitic groups in Austria, in the decade before World War I, as an emblem of "Aryan" racial purity). But the swastika was also associated with many other divinities, including Christ, in catacomb inscriptions. In Jainism, it signified the supreme being.

See also:

843 Mortality and Transcience, p.36
844 Power, p.88

845-6 THUNDER AND LIGHTNING

Thunder (845) and **lightning (846)** were symbolically linked with many sky gods. In the Book of Exodus, they represent the presence of God proclaiming the Ten Commandments: thunder symbolizes the divine voice, lightning his written word. The thunderbolt, often shown in the form of jagged arrows, is the emblem of divine authority in the hand of Zeus (Jupiter) in the Greco-Roman pantheon, and of other powerful male gods such as the Scandinavian Thor. Alternatively, as in North America and Southern Africa, the divine might of thunder and lightning was personified by a giant bird of prey, in

See also:

845-6 Fertility (Water) pp.49–50

847 Mortality and Transience p.36

America the Thunderbird. People touched by lightning
were once thought to bear the mark of God.

847 WIND

Wind gods were important deities in many cultures,
particularly in pre-Columbian America. But currents of air
have more general and subtle symbolism as a metaphor for
the nature of divinity – a force that can be felt but not seen,
invisible but permeating all things. In Christianity, wind has
been taken as a symbol of the Holy Ghost in the second verse
of the Book of Genesis: "And the earth was without form, and
void; and darkness was upon the face of the deep. And the
Spirit of God moved upon the face of the waters."

848 CROSS

Salvation is the primary symbolism of the Christian cross, in addition to its role as the emblem of faith. It represents redemption from sin through the sacrifice of the man-god Jesus, and the promise of eternal life to those who believe in him. The traditional cross has one transverse bar near the top of the upright shaft, and this is also the usual form of the **crucifix (849)**, which adds to the plain cross the figure of a man hanging from the bar. But there are ten other major cross forms with different shades of meaning, together with hundreds of heraldic forms.

A short bar above the centrally placed main bar of the **Greek cross (850)** refers to the ironic inscription nailed above Jesus by the Romans: INRI – an acronym for "Jesus of Nazareth, King of the Jews". This double-bar form became known as the Cross of Lorraine.

See also:

848
Protection,
p.22

855
Innocence
(Lamb),
p.164

The **Y-shaped cross (851)** worn on priestly robes is a graphic summary of Jesus hanging from his raised arms. This shape has been associated with the image of a man hanging on the **Tree of Life (852)**, an ancient symbol of regeneration through the sacrifice of a human scapegoat. Jesus is shown crucified on a tree rather than a cross in some medieval paintings.

The early Christian cross form known as the **Chi-Rho (853)** may also have had salvational meaning for troops of the Emperor Constantine who carried this emblem into battle in 312CE. Formed from the Greek letters XP, it was an acronym not only of "Christ" but also of "chreston", meaning a good omen, giving it talismanic as well as spiritual significance.

In Egypt, the Coptic Church interpreted the **Ankh (854)**, an ancient cross form topped by a loop, as a symbol of eternal life through Christ, the loop signifying continuity.

855 AGNUS DEI

The Agnus Dei ("Lamb of God") is an emblem showing a lamb with a cross or cross-shaped halo topped by a banner symbolizing victory over death through the sacrificial saviour, Jesus. The blood of the lambs sacrificed in Jerusalem at Passover was already an established Hebrew symbol of salvation at the time of Christ's death.

856 ANCHOR

The anchor was not only an early Christian secret sign for the cross but was also used by St Paul as a symbol of salvation through its wider significance as a vital instrument of safety at sea in stormy weather. In Hebrews 6:19, the apostle tells beleaguered Christian sects to rely on salvation as "an anchor of the soul, both sure and steadfast".

857 DOLPHIN

A dolphin pierced by a trident or combined with an anchor was another early Christian symbol of salvation through Christ. Mediterranean legends and myths concerning dolphins who had saved human beings played an important part in the establishment of this symbolism. The dolphin was also thought by some to be the "great fish" that swallowed Jonah and, as a result of this, an analogy was made between this story and Christ's death and resurrection.

See also:
857 Death, p.300

858 ARK

In medieval sacred art, Noah's ark sometimes appears as a symbol of the saving doctrines of the Church; Jesus, as the great redeemer, is himself equated with the ark as humanity's salvation.

859–60 GRAPES AND BLOOD

On Christian graves, bunches of **grapes (859)** are emblems of redemption and salvation. The symbolic association between the grape and divine blessing is very old. In the Bible, a vine branch bearing grapes was the first sign that the Israelis had reached the Promised Land. Christianity inherited this symbolism and gave it new meaning by linking Jesus with the vine and wine with his sacrificial **blood (860)**. In Jesus' words, "I am the true vine and my Father is the vinegrower". His blood, washing away sin, is the emblematic means of Christian salvation.

861 GRAIL

Medieval legends and romances of the quest for the Grail have left scholars in disagreement about its symbolism,

See also:

859 Fecundity and Plenty, p.63

860 Duality and Union, p.289

861 Mortality and Transience (Cup), p.37

but in Christian thinking it is the search for God's grace – the ultimate source of salvation – through a mystic personal communion with Christ. Hence suggestions that the Holy Grail is the chalice used at the Last Supper, or a lost cup containing the blood of Jesus collected by Joseph of Arimathea during Jesus' crucifixion.

862 SPRING

The purity symbolism of water from natural springs gave birth to ancient myths of a spring at the base of the Tree of Life which washed away sins. An image of four streams issuing from such a spring and flowing through Paradise is a Christian symbol of salvation. Among desert peoples, the **well (863)** was an ancient emblem of salvation, as in the biblical story of God revealing a well to Hagar and her son Ishmael who were dying of thirst after Abraham cast them out into the wilderness. The link between water and salvation is one aspect of the Christian baptism, though this is primarily a rite of purification.

IMAGES OF THE SOUL

864 SOUL PERSONIFIED

Classical images of the soul show it as a small fluttering figure entering the body at birth and leaving it at death. In Greek mythology, **Psyche (865)**, literally meaning "soul", is the most famous personification of the belief that humans possess an indwelling spirit of this sort. According to the Roman writer Apuleius, the beautiful Psyche wins immortality through her all-consuming love for the god Eros. The link between the soul and love has been influential ever since.

866 BUTTERFLY

In art, Psyche is often shown with butterfly wings. The parallel between the butterfly emerging in splendour from the dark chrysalis and the soul leaving the body after death appears to have occurred to many cultures. Images of butterflies as souls have been found as far apart as Africa, Central Asia, Mexico and New Zealand. They have the same symbolism on Christian tombs and in paintings in which the Christ child holds a butterfly in his hand.

See also:

866 Enlightenment and Transformation, p.347

868 Sovereignty, p.107

867 BIRDS

The almost universal link between birds and the spiritual
side of human nature makes them the most common
symbols of the soul. The hierarchy of birds suggested to
the Romans that an **eagle (868)** should be released from
the pyre of an emperor in order to symbolize his passage
to the afterlife.

In common with many other
cultures, the Egyptians believed
that an individual had several souls.
The spiritual element which left the
body at death was the **Ba (869)**,
depicted as a human-headed hawk. The
Ka (870), which symbolized the personality
of the deceased, remained beside the
body in the form of a funerary statue.

871 THE MYSTIC SPARK

A number of mystical traditions which see the universe in
dualistic terms of light and darkness hold that human beings
contain within them a spark of the divine spirit, perceived
as light itself. At death, this spiritual energy can free itself
of the material body that briefly contained it and return to
the godhead.

This concept of humans sharing in a universal soul can be traced in Orphic, Gnostic and Cabbalistic thought. A Cabbalist sign for the divine spark within the material body was a circle within a square.

There are similarities with Indian philosophical and religious traditions of a **cosmic soul (872)**, imperfect elements of which are reincarnated in the material world.

873 LIZARD

The lizard's ability to shed its skin, and sometimes also its tail, and resume its form associated it in some cultures with rebirth and with the soul. This seems to account for its use as a motif on church censers and candle-holders. Superstition claimed that souls in lizard form could dart from the mouth of a sleeping person and return before daybreak, recalling old Arab beliefs that the soul left the body during sleep.

See also:

873 Purification, Atonement and Propitiation (Salamander), p.361

IMMORTALITY AND ETERNITY

874 TOMB ARCHITECTURE

Immortality, in the sense of a continuing life on the spiritual plane, is asserted symbolically by many kinds of megalithic tombs or tomb markers, such as the thousands of massive flat-topped burial chambers or **dolmens (875)** and upright standing stones called **menhirs (876)** built across north-western Europe in the Neolithic and early Bronze Ages. Images and artefacts associated with them suggest cults of mother figures, heroes and ancestors whose spirits lived on and whose help or protection was invoked by these monuments.

The Egyptian **pyramid (877)**, the most powerful architectural emblem of immortality, was specifically designed to symbolize the union between the buried pharaoh and the undying sun. Its originating architect, Imhotep, was high priest of the sun-god Ra. His pyramid for the pharaoh Zozer at Saqqara was stepped in the manner of ziggurats, but later builders filled in and faced their pyramids with limestone to reflect the sun's light and strengthen both the structure and its symbolism as "material for eternity".

878 MOON

The moon's ability to vanish and reappear made it a symbol of immortality almost everywhere, and linked it with myths of the death and rebirth of gods as well as humans. Its crescent sometimes appears with this symbolism in funerary art, as on Islamic graves where it is shown with the Tree of Life. Chinese legend said that it was under a laurel tree on the moon that the **lunar hare (879)** mixed the elixir of immortality.

880 FRUIT

Immortality gained by eating a magical fruit or herb is a common theme in mythology and legend. A constant feature of these stories is the rarity of immortality and the difficulty of winning it. One of the "12 labours" of Herakles in classical mythology was to bring back **golden apples (881)** from the western garden of the Hesperides (the daughters of Night). The apples grow on a tree guarded by a fearsome snake and, in one version of the myth, Herakles persuades the Titan Atlas to fetch them while he takes over the duty of holding up the world. The garden is death and the apples immortality. In almost reverse symbolism, Adam and Eve are cast out from the garden of immortality for eating an apple from a snake-entwined tree.

In Chinese mythology, the fruit of immortality is the **peach (882)** – a popular motif on Chinese porcelain for this reason. The Queen of Heaven was said to own a peach Tree of Immortality which blossomed only once every 3,000 years and produced the sacred ripe fruit 3,000 years later.

883–91 PLANTS AND TREES

The Babylonian epic of the hero Gilgamesh tells of how he meets an Immortal on the far side of the Waters of Death who informs him of a magic **herb (883)** at the bottom of the sea. He finds it, but it is then stolen by a **snake (884)**, which uses it to rejuvenate itself by shedding its skin.

The herb may have been the aromatic bay species of **laurel (885)**, once widely associated with magical powers. Its links with immortality help to explain why the laurel wreath became the emblem of victors whose names deserved to live forever. In China, the laurel is a rival to the peach as the Tree of Immortality. A hallucinogenic **mushroom (886)** was also said to be the food of Chinese Immortals.

Amaranth (887), the name for a number of hardy flowering plants, was a common motif on Greek tombs as an emblem of

See also:

878 Fertility, p.44; Femininity and Maternity, p.123

879 Fertility, p.48

882 Truth and Deceit, p.168

884 Protection, p.30; Evil, p.155

885 Health, p.85

immortality. In the Chinese Moon Festival, it was symbolically offered to the lunar hare with the same meaning.

Immortality is also symbolized in China by the **ginkgo (888)**, believed to be the oldest of all tree species to have survived unchanged. It was grown around temples for this reason. Resinous conifers also have ancient associations with immortality. Consequently, the **pine (889)** was planted on or near Chinese graves, as the **cypress (890)** often is in Western tradition. In Judeo-Christian tradition, **acacia (891)** was a symbol of immortality; the *shittah* used to build the Israelite Tabernacle is said to have been an acacia species of hardwood.

892–3 SOMA AND MEAD

Soma (892), a narcotic drink possibly produced from the mushroom *Amaniti muscaria*, played a central role in ancient Vedic and Hindu rites of sacrifice and purification.

Personified by a god of the same name, it was the nectar of immortality in Indian tradition. An aim of Hatha Yoga is to channel energy up through the spine in such a way that the adept's body is emptied of the poison of illusion and then refilled by a spiritual soma coursing down from the highest level of consciousness. Only complete identification with

See also:

894 Sovereignty, p.103; Vigilance and Guardianship, p.140; Gluttony, Sloth, Avarice and Pride, p.193

the universal spirit could lead to immortality.

In Celtic tradition, **mead (893)** was the preferred drink of the gods and the nectar of immortality. It was made from fermented honey, mixed with spices and water and was probably similar to the ambrosia which in Greek legend was drunk by the Immortals.

894 PEACOCK

Awe and unfamiliarity with this bird in the ancient world led to a legend that its flesh was incorruptible. This may have been a factor in its glorification in Roman imperial ceremonials and in its becoming an emblem of immortality

895 CICADA

Jade cicadas were sometimes buried with the dead in China as emblems of immortality. The same symbolism appears in the Greek myth of Tithonus, a mortal kept alive by an ambrosia provided by the goddess of dawn, Eos (Aurora), who loved him. Finding that she could stop him dying but not from ageing, she eventually took pity on his decrepitude and turned him into an immortal cicada. The symbolism seems to have been based on the insect's longevity, despite its dessicated appearance.

REBIRTH AND RESURRECTION

896 PHOENIX

This mythical creature is the most famous of all rebirth symbols. Greek and Roman writers reported that the phoenix was a lone male bird which lived for 500 years and then immolated itself on a fragrant nest set alight by the heat of the sun. From its ashes rose a newly born phoenix which would carry the nest to Heliopolis, the central city of Egyptian sun worship, and dedicate it to the sun god, Ra.

Originally, the phoenix may have been a poetic emblem of the rising sun, based on the **heron (897)**, which had ancient solar and ascensional symbolism in Egypt. But as its legend developed, Christianity saw an analogy with the story of Christ's resurrection three days after his crucifixion. The phoenix can appear with this meaning beside the cross in medieval paintings of the Crucifixion, and sometimes on tombs. It is obvious that artists were uncertain about its form and it often appears, ringed with fire, looking more like an eagle than a heron.

See also:

896 War and Victory, p.278

898 Purity and Incorruptibility, p.217

Fire (898) itself has regeneration symbolism, as can be seen from Christian Easter rituals in which candles are first extinguished and then relit from a "new fire". In Christian funerary art, an urn with a flame issuing from its top is a resurrection symbol.

899 RESURRECTION GODS

The resurrection of vegetation gods after their death and disintegration provides an important symbolic theme in many ancient mythologies, paralleling the dying, hacking down and regrowth of plant life.

Osiris in Egypt and Dionysus in Greece are famous examples of gods who were said to have been torn to pieces as a prelude to their rebirth. These traditions formed a basis for several mystery religions in the Roman Empire which rivalled Christianity in offering rituals that symbolized the washing away of sin, salvation by a redeeming god and reincarnation. Some of the later symbolism of the vine god, Dionysus, suggests syncretic borrowings between the New Testament and the mystery cult of Orphism in which Dionysus was established as the most important figure.

A primitive symbol of the process of disintegration and rebirth was **dismemberment (900)**, a form of sacrifice practised by earlier followers of Dionysus in Asia Minor. This involved tearing apart animals or humans and eating the flesh raw, mimicking a Phrygian myth in which the god himself was torn apart by Titans.

See also:

901 Fertility, p.46

901   MAYPOLE

The maypole probably originated in Greek and Roman resurrection rites of another "dying god", Attis. In a Phrygian myth, this youth was driven mad by the jealous Earth Mother, Cybele, castrated himself and died. To invoke his resurrection, cult followers of Cybele wound woollen bands around a bare pine tree and danced beneath it each spring. The custom of dancing around a pole was incorporated into the Roman festival of Hilaria, and later spread into the Celtic world.

902   OUROBOROS

Death and rebirth is part of the symbolism of the *ouroboros*, a circular image of a snake swallowing its own tail. In the Greek cult of Orphism, the blank space

See also:

904 Power, p.88

906 Fertility,
p.44; Femininity
and Maternity,
p.123

909 Wealth and
Prosperity, p.65

908 Temperance
and Humility,
p.189

encircled by the snake's body stood for the egg of reincarnation. In its religious Egyptian form, the emblem is thought to have represented the circular journey of the sun, entering the underworld at night and reappearing each morning. And in Gnostic thought, it suggested the endless cycle of Nature, constantly recreating itself. The image suggests eternity, self-sufficiency and renewal.

The **snake (903)** itself was almost everywhere associated with reincarnation and rejuvenation through its ability to shed its skin.

904–5 WHEEL AND DISK

In Hindu and Buddhist art, the **wheel (904)** symbolizes the cycles of manifestation – birth, death and rebirth. The **disk (905),** or solid wheel as it was before the invention of spokes, represented resurrection to a new life in Egypt by association with the circular return or rebirth of the sun.

906 MOON

The moon's constantly changing aspect and, in particular, its complete disappearance for three days (known as the "dark of the moon") made it the most impressive natural symbol of the cosmic and earthly cycles of birth, growth, decline, death and rebirth. In some traditions, it was an entrance to the afterlife, or the transitory home of the illustrious dead who were destined to be reborn and to return to the earth.

907–8 BONES AND ASH

Bones (907) were symbols of resurrection as well as death in many ancient cultures, which often accounts for the care with which they were protected in burial chambers as the material most likely to survive and be of use in a future life. This was true not only of human skeletons but of animal bones, which were often buried with the dead to ensure that they would have game to hunt when they rose again. Ash (908) was also used as a symbol of rebirth, particularly in North American Indian custom.

909 EGG

Throughout the world, the egg is a central symbol of recreation as well as creation. It stands for Christ's resurrection both in Easter ceremonials and in the folk tradition of giving chocolate eggs.

In the Greek cult of Orphism, notable for its belief in the concept of salvation and the immortality of the soul, the egg symbolized the hope of reincarnation. There are images of a figure representing the resurrection god, Dionysus, holding an egg in his hand.

910 WHALE

The story of Jonah and the whale became a popular medieval allegory of the resurrection of Christ. With this symbolism, scenes of Jonah being disgorged by the "great fish" appear not only in paintings and stained glass but also in early Christian funerary art. According to Matthew, Jesus told his disciples that he would go down into the earth for three days and three nights, just as Jonah had spent this period of time in the belly of the fish. In this way the whale became a symbol not only of death but also of deliverance from death. The period of three days and three nights seems to have clear lunar associations with the "dark of the moon" and its reappearance.

See also:

912 Fame and Fortune, p.73

911 OCTAGON

The eight-sided form of the Christian baptistry is a symbol of rebirth to eternal life. The octagon was perceived as a form mediating between the square (symbolizing earth) and the circle (symbolizing heaven), and therefore implying a spiritual rite of passage. In the arcane lore of numbers, **eight (912)** was itself a symbol of renewal, as it followed the so-called "complete" number, seven, and started a new cycle.

913 EAST

Churches, mosques and, often, graves are orientated towards the east because this direction of space is traditionally associated not only with solar light and divinity but also with new life and therefore the hope of resurrection, particularly in Christian thought. Islamic worshippers face east to signify that they are spiritually aligned to the divine source.

914 SCARAB

An ancient emblem of cyclic renewal, the scarab or dung beetle became an early Christian symbol of resurrection.

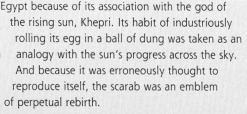

It had been for centuries the most popular amulet of Egypt because of its association with the god of the rising sun, Khepri. Its habit of industriously rolling its egg in a ball of dung was taken as an analogy with the sun's progress across the sky. And because it was erroneously thought to reproduce itself, the scarab was an emblem of perpetual rebirth.

915 BEE

The bee is a symbol of reincarnation in India and was sometimes carved on tombs as a resurrection emblem This symbolism seems to have been based on the winter habit of bees staying in the hive, misread as a death phase followed by their mass reappearance in spring.

916 LOTUS

The lotus had rebirth as well as creation symbolism in ancient cultures ranging from the Middle East to Mexico. It is sometimes found in Greco-Roman funerary art with the same significance.

917 NARCISSUS

This is the flower of Persephone in the Greek myth of her abduction by the lord of the underworld while she was innocently picking its blooms. As she was allowed to return to the earth each spring, it was used in the rites of her grain goddess mother, Demeter, and planted on graves as a rebirth emblem symbolizing the idea that death is only a sleep.

918 CORN

Corn was a funerary emblem of regeneration and rebirth throughout all the regions that depended on wheat, barley or maize as a staple crop. A consecrated ear of corn, the attribute of Demeter, was central to the drama of the great mystery cycles performed at Eleusis near Athens, standing for the miracle of spring regrowth from grain seeds left by the harvest. Wheat remains a significant Christian symbol of resurrection, based on the New Testament passage from John: "Unless a grain of wheat falls in the earth and dies, it remains just a single grain; but if it dies it bears much fruit".

See also:

915 Sovereignty, p.106

916 Beauty and Grace, p.132

918 Fertility, p.51

ENLIGHTENMENT AND TRANSFORMATION

919 FLOWER

An influential story of Gautama Buddha is that he was asked by his disciples to describe enlightenment and simply held up a flower, turning it in his fingers and smiling. The transcendent non-answer of the "Flower Sermon" symbolized a state beyond verbal definition.

The flower particularly associated with enlightenment is the **lotus (920)**, an emblem of unfolding spiritual wisdom. It is a symbol of the Buddha's own nature and he is often shown enthroned on a fully-opened flower representing *nirvana*, or final release from the wheel of being. The unfolded lotus is also a symbol of ultimate light in Taoism and ultimate purity in Hinduism.

921 CIRCUMAMBULATION

Progress toward enlightenment is symbolized in Buddhist thought by circumambulation around a temple, a ritual thought to place the worshipper in tune with cosmic rhythms. In both Hinduism and Buddhism, the direction is traditionally clockwise, following the path seemingly taken by the sun around the earth. At Mecca, Muslims symbolically approach the Seventh Heaven by circumambulations in the

opposite direction, following
the polar wheel of the stars.

See also:

920 Beauty and Grace,
p.132; Rebirth and
Resurrection, p.338

922 SHAPE CHANGING

The concept of spiritual transformation or liberation from
the material plane of existence is often symbolized by shape
changing, a sign of supernatural power in countless legends
and myths where divinities transmogrify into animals at will.
Animal skins, bird masks and similar disguises used by shamans
and magicians were worn as emblems of their ability to
change shape, transcend nature and visit realms of the spirit.

923 ALCHEMY

The ancient pseudo-science of alchemy symbolized humanity's belief that it was itself capable of discovering a way to
transform imperfect matter into perfect spirit – not through
religion or techniques of meditation, but through chemistry.
The theory was that, since the elements of matter can change
their form, it should be possible to boil them down to an
original essence (*materia prima*) and then use the unifying
and transforming power of **fire (924)** to create, step by step,
a mysterious catalyst called the **philosopher's stone (925)**
which could turn base metals to gold and, on the spiritual
plane, produce enlightenment from human baseness.

The metal most associated with transformation was **mercury (926)**, also known as "liquid silver", because of its ability to form easy amalgams with other metals. In China, mercury was linked with the dragon and with the liquid bodily elements of blood, semen and water; it also had transformation symbolism in India as a metaphor for the yogic flow of spiritual energy.

927 WATER

Water, like fire, is an ancient symbol of transformation. This is the emblematic meaning of the great **Flood (928)**, which

appears in Mesopotamian mythology before the biblical account of Noah and the ark was written. Human crimes, injustices and follies are dissolved back into the original deep from which life emerged, leading to a fresh start and the emergence of a civilization with a clean moral slate.

929 CAVE

Caves are magical places in mythology and legend, and there are many tales of people wandering into them and

See also:

927 Purity and Incorruptibility, p.218; Instinct, Intuition and the Unconscious, p.262

See also:

934 Death, p.300;
Salvation and
Redemption, p.319

emerging transformed. Their ancient use in
initiation rites may account for this, the cave
becoming a symbol for a descent into the
grave followed by a "rebirth" in wisdom or
maturity. Clefts or caves were often sites for
oracles. A Greek cave at Lebadea was said to possess the
ability to pull underground those people who put their feet
in a cleft, returning them in a state of enlightenment.

930 INITIATION

Transformation from one state of life to another is the symbolism of initiation, a rite of passage with ancient roots and
known in nearly all societies. Although the rites can vary
dramatically, they have as their basis the idea of a symbolic
"death" followed by a rebirth. More primitive rites took this
as far as heaping earth over candidates; others mimed
the passage of the initiate through the body of a creature
associated with transformation, such as the **snake (931)**.

Circumcision (932) was an ancient ritual of initiation and
transformation in many societies even where, as in Jewish
custom, it was performed on infants, partly for hygienic reasons and partly to mark their status as one of God's "chosen
people". In Liberia, where circumcision was part of the initiation rite at puberty, scars on the penises of the initiates were

said to be the marks of a **crocodile (933)** which had swallowed them as boys and returned them as adults.

934 DOLPHIN

The affinity between humans and dolphins made this creature a symbol of transformation in Greco-Roman legends. It was associated particularly with Dionysus (Bacchus) who was said to change himself into a dolphin in order to carry Cretan worshippers to his shrine at Delphi. The dolphin is an alternative to the whale as the "great fish" which swallows Jonah in the biblical transformation myth of this prophet.

935 WINE

In ancient religious rituals, wine was often a central emblem of spiritual transformation because the process by which it developed over time from the juice of crushed grapes seemed mysterious, almost magical, and because it also changed those who drank it. A symbolic transformation from the human state into the ever-energized state of divinity was the object of the orgiastic wine-drinking rites associated with the worship of Dionysus (Bacchus).

In a significant New Testament sequence, Jesus works his first miracle by changing water into wine at a wedding feast in Cana, then suggests at the Last Supper a deeper spiritual

transformation from wine to his own
blood, shed to redeem humanity.

See also:

938 Images of
the Soul, p.322

936 BRIDGE

The bridge often appears as a symbol of transition and
transformation, marking a decisive break between one state
and another. In Indo-Iranian mythology, Chinvat Parvatu,
the Bridge of the Separator, symbolized the difficulty of
negotiating the transformation from death to the afterlife.
Like the hair's breadth Islamic bridge to paradise, it was so
narrow that only the souls of the righteous could cross it
without toppling into hell.

The Pope's title of pontiff is taken over from the
Pontifex Maximus (Chief Bridge-Builder) of
the pagan priesthood of Rome

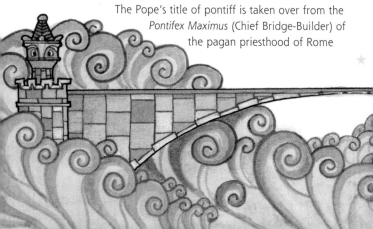

who, like the Pope, was the symbolic architect of
the passage from the material to the spiritual plane.

937–8 FROG AND BUTTERFLY

In legend and folklore, the **frog (937)** is a popular symbol
of transformation, not only because of its impressive switch
from tadpole to talkative amphibian but also because of its
humanoid features. Hence the Brothers Grimm fairytale of a
frog turning into a handsome prince and many other stories
in which people are transformed into frogs, or vice-versa.

While the frog represents evolution on the physical plane,
the **butterfly (938)**, changing from a wormlike caterpillar
to a creature of ethereal beauty, is the natural
world's most poetic symbol of physi-
cal-spiritual transformation.

ASCENSION AND AXIAL INTERCHANGE

939   AXIS MUNDI

A constant feature of ancient cosmologies is the idea of a vertical force field, spindle or axis around which the universe revolves and which provides a conduit for the flow of divine energy between the three spheres of underworld, earth and heavens. The many symbols of this *axis mundi* range from features of the natural world to the columnar structure of the human backbone, conceived in Indian philosophies as a channel for redirecting physical and sensual energy into spiritual energy.

940   MOUNTAIN

The supernatural aura of great mountains towering into mist made them mythical abodes of gods and Immortals (as in the Greek Olympus), places of revelation (as in the Bible) and powerful symbols both of centrality and of spiritual ascent (as in Indian, Chinese and Japanese mythologies). Most major cultures had a sacred mountain which was emblematically the axial centre of the world, even if it existed only in the imagination.

In the Bible, it is on mountains that God speaks to Moses and Elijah, on a mount that Jesus delivers his most famous

sermon and from the Mount of Olives that Acts suggests
he ascended to heaven (other hills that have been suggested
are Mount Tabor and Mount Hermon). In Hindu and Jain
mythology, the centre of the universe is Mount Meru, a
golden mountain lying somewhere beyond the Himalayas,
spreading upward and outward like a lotus.

941 LADDER

Jacob's dream in Genesis of a ladder
that extended from earth to heaven,
upon which angels descended
and ascended, echoes ancient
beliefs that a direct means of
communication between gods
and humans existed in an earlier
age but was lost through human
fault. English Romantic and
Pre-Raphaelite artists took up
this symbolism in paintings

that posed dreamy-faced maidens on celestial staircases.

Celestial ladders appear in many other traditions, from Egypt and the Islamic world through Asia to North America. Seven stages of ascent are often represented, suggesting an association with planetary symbolism.

942 STEPPED TEMPLES

Ancient stepped temples embody the aspirational symbolism of the mountain. The Babylonian **ziggurat (943)** rose in a series of layers representing stages of spiritual progress and provided at the top a sanctuary dedicated to a particular god who was invited to descend to it.

Still vaster "mountains of the gods" were built by Hindu architects, especially in South East Asia, symbolizing the principle of cosmic ascension towards a divine pavilion ruled over by Shiva, as at Angkor Wat. In the original Buddhist form of the **stupa (944)** in India, the rising tiers symbolized the successive stages by which the Buddha renounced the material world, and a central mast piercing the temple from top to bottom represented the Bodhi Tree under which he attained enlightenment. This axial shaft is a feature of the Asian **pagoda (945)**, which often has parasol-like discs near the summit. Parasols once had royal symbolism but here they represent celestial spheres.

946 POLE STAR

For many civilizations, the bright and steady light of the North Star in the constellation of Ursa Minor was the symbolic axis of the turning world. Some cultures revered it as a divinity or believed it was the summit of a supernatural pole drawing souls to heaven or channelling divine power downwards. For peoples of the far north, it was the cosmic navel.

947 TREE OF LIFE

A mythical Tree of Life or World Tree rooted in the underworld and stretching far into the sky appears in a remarkable number of traditions as a symbol of cosmic unity, cyclic regeneration and constant, dynamic interchange between matter and spirit, earth and heaven. With these emblematic meanings, the giant **ash (948)**, called Yggdrasil, became a focal point of Scandinavian mythology. Animist beliefs that trees were magical living spirits undoubtedly played a part in this concept of the world axis. So did the allusive form of a spreading tree, its branches suggesting evolution and aspiration. Some images of the World Tree show it inverted, its roots drawing spiritual nourishment from the sky and channelling it downwards.

Whether a noble **cedar (949)**, as in Sumeria, or a fruiting tree such as the **fig (950)**

See also:

947 Longevity, p.40

in Egypt, the Tree of Life symbolized the belief that human beings could transcend their natural state and reach out to the divine. In some myths, **supernatural birds (951)** nesting in the branches were guiding intermediaries between sky and earth. Alternatively, springs of wisdom, rejuvenation or spiritual nourishment flowed from the tree's base.

952 MANDORLA

In medieval paintings the ascension from earth to heaven of sacred figures, particularly Christ and the Virgin Mary, is often symbolized by enclosing them in an almond-shaped frame called the mandorla. The origin of this device is disputed, some thinking it evolved from an oval halo. But the almond has strong symbolic links with virgin birth and purity. Its opposing arcs can also represent duality and the gateway from earthly to celestial life.

953 INCENSE

The burning of scented woods, resins and gums has been seen as a means of communicating with gods for thousands of years. The custom, known from Egypt to the easternmost shores of Asia, began as a practical measure to sweeten the air at funerals or in religious ceremonies involving animal sacrifices or other burnt offerings. But before long it took on a symbolic importance of its own, effectively becoming a medium of prayer in the visible form of fragrant ascending smoke. Two of the traditional gifts that were brought to Jesus by the Magi – frankincense and myrrh – were not only valuable commodities in the ancient world, but were also symbols of worship.

See also:

953 Purity and Incorruptibility, p.220

954 CREMATION

In Indo-Iranian tradition, cremation symbolizes the final release of the soul from the body, with fire and flame standing for purification and smoke for ascension.

955–8 RAINBOW AND CELESTIAL CREATURES

The **rainbow (955)** appears in many cultures as a ladder or bridge between the temporal and the spiritual. This explains why Christ is sometimes shown seated on a rainbow in sacred art. The Greek rainbow goddess, Iris, was a messenger divinity. Rainbow ribbons worn by Turkic shamans were emblematic signs of their ability to visit higher realms of knowledge. In Tantric Buddhism, the "rainbow body" describes the ultimate transitional state of the adept as the corporeal begins to dissolve into pure spirit.

The rainbow was associated with a cosmic **serpent (956)** in African, Indian, Asian and Australian traditions – the snake itself is a major symbol of axial and ascensional powers. It appears nearly everywhere as a magico-religious link between the underworld and earth, and in imagery is sometimes given celestial symbolism by the addition of wings or feathers. The most notable example of this is the Aztec god Quetzalcoatl, a **plumed serpent (957)**

See also:

955 Wealth, p.67

whose mythical powers enable him to intervene in under-world, earthly and celestial affairs, and who was said to have finally become the planet Venus. In Asia, the celestial man-date of the dragon is indicated by its **eagle claws (958).**

959 OMPHALOS

A Greek image of the world axis or centre was the sacred stone of the famous oracle of Apollo at Delphi, called the *omphalos* (navel). A short column with an ovoid top covered in a network of tracery, it represented an umbilical cord con-necting the living with the dead and with the divine – both potential sources of occult wisdom. Another *omphalos* in Crete was said to mark the spot where the umbilical cord of Zeus had fallen.

Similar stones representing a world centre are known from other cultures, notably Judaism and Islam. For both faiths, the rock on which Jerusalem is built has sacred significance as a kind of spiritual navel.

960 ROPE

Ascension towards enlightenment is the symbolism of the Indian rope trick, the rope becoming an emblem of the Hindu belief that spiritual discipline can arouse a sleeping serpent, *kundalini*, coiled at the base of the spine, and produce a flow of life-force rising in a steadily purified form to the highest centre of consciousness. Rope and serpent were interlinked in the ancient Vedic myth of a cosmic serpent acting like a rope to twirl a mountain and churn life from the milky sea of creation.

961–2 WHIRLWIND AND CHARIOT

The spiralling **whirlwind (961)**, literally an ascensional force in its most destructive form, was widely seen as a manifestation of the divine spirit and a dynamic example of the single unifying energy pervading the whole cosmos. A remarkable passage of the Old Testament (Kings II: 1:11) marries divine power to the power of human technology in the story of the prophet Elijah who was walking with a friend when: "behold, there appeared a chariot of fire, and horses of fire, and parted them both asunder, and Elijah went up by a whirlwind into heaven".

Taking the **chariot (962)** as a symbol of spiritual ascent, Jewish Merhabah mystics of the 2nd century sought to contemplate the throne of God by the means of passing into trance states that would then allow their spirits to be whirled upward to travel through space in a similar manner.

See also:

962 Authority, p.100

PURIFICATION, ATONEMENT AND PROPITIATION

963 BAPTISM

Symbolic purification has been a major element in religious rituals of initiation in almost all cultures. The emblematic associations of **water (964)** with dissolution and regeneration or rebirth made it the most commonly used medium in countries of the Middle East, where the relative scarcity of water gave it even higher value. Islamic purification rituals of **washing (965)** are part of daily worship.

Christian baptism (which replaced circumcision as an initiatory rite when the Christian religion broke away from Judaism) was made prescriptive through the words of Jesus in the Gospel of John: "Unless one is born of water and the Spirit, he cannot enter the kingdom of God". This added the gift of divine grace (the Spirit) to the purification symbolism of the Christian rite, which represents the dissolving of past sins and rebirth from the original waters of life. Although repentance was preached by John the Baptist, this later became a less significant aspect of baptismal symbolism than purification and regeneration.

See also:

966 Purity and Incorruptibility p.217; Divinity and Sanctity, p.308

968 Grief, Mourning and Melancholia (Ritual Actions), p.259

966 FIRE

Fire is the ultimate symbol of purification, and a dangerous one, as shown not only by the burning of heretics, witches and others accused of being evil doers during the Christian era, but also by some fire cults of the ancient world where human victims were sacrificed. In a non-symbolic sense, fire is of course a powerful agent of purification – for example, it was largely responsible for wiping out a devastating plague at the time of the Great Fire of London. Fire's symbolic meaning of spiritual purification survives in the Roman Catholic doctrine of **Purgatory (967)**, a place of undefined location in which the venial sins of those who are not yet considered fit to enter heaven directly are said to be burned away. In art, St Teresa is shown interceding with Christ to release these poor souls from the flames in which they stand.

968 FASTING

Purification is an aspect of most forms of fasting, particularly in Jainism, Hinduism and Taoism, where it is linked to the progressive shedding of earthly attachments. Atonement through self-denial is more commonly the symbolism of the three major religious fasts of Ramadan in Islam, Lent in Christianity and Yom Kippur in Judaism.

Many lesser food restrictions can symbolize purification, notably the **unleavened bread (969)**, traditionally eaten at the Jewish Passover.

970 FLAGELLATION

Flagellation was only one of many self-inflicted punishments used in the ancient world by religious followers as a symbol of atonement or purification. It reached almost epidemic proportions among Christian sects in the later Middle Ages before the Church decided it was heretical and forbid it.

971 METALLURGY

Ancient beliefs that metals trapped in the earth were of cosmic origin led to early metallurgy becoming a symbol of spiritual testing and purification. A parallel was made between metals and humans as earthly things with celestial potential. This idea underlaid the whole symbolism of alchemy, which sought to transform base metals into silver and gold. These two substances stood at the apex of a cosmic hierarchy in which seven metals were associated with the seven known "planets". With gold standing for the sun and silver for the moon, the other five in descending order were: mercury for Mercury, copper for Venus, iron for Mars, tin for Jupiter and lead for Saturn.

972 SALAMANDER

The mythical salamander, depicted in medieval art as a lizard surrounded by flames, was said to be able to extinguish fire. Known from ancient legends, it became a popular alchemical symbol for the two purifying agents, fire and sulphur. The Church took up this symbolism by using the salamander as an emblem of the pure-spirited Christian, able to resist the fires of sensuality. It is possible that the basis for the legend may have been the small, brightly marked amphibian called the fire salamander – it has red and yellow skin and lives in damp habitats.

See also:

972 Images of the Soul (Lizard), p.324

973 SIEVE

The large sieves used in the ancient world to sift grain from dirt and husks became a biblical symbol of divine judgement and the process of purification by which only the righteous would reach heaven. This explains why allegorical figures such as Chastity and Prudence may hold a sieve in some Christian paintings.

974 SACRIFICE

Religious sacrifice is a symbol of atonement or propitiation in which something of value is offered to a divinity, usually after rites in which the offering is purified or sanctified. In the ancient world, offerings ranged from simple gifts of food or oblations of wine to the ritual slaughter of **animals (975)** or, in the most extreme form of sacrifice, **humans (976)**. The biblical story of Abraham's readiness to sacrifice his own **son (977)**, Isaac, at divine command is followed in later books of the Old Testament by frequent criticisms of child sacrifices carried out by kings of Judah.

In Mexico as late as the beginning of the 16th century, an estimated 20,000 victims a year were sacrificed to the sun god Huitzilopochtli by the rulers of the Aztec Empire. The symbolic basis of this horrific

See also:

978 Duality and Union, p.289

979 Fertility, p.47

cult was the myth that the Aztecs were a people chosen to provide the sun god with the nourishing power of human **blood (978)**, necessary to enable the sun to renew its daily struggle against darkness.

As it possessed in the Christian Eucharist, blood had ritual significance in many sacrificial customs as a symbol of spiritual life. In the Roman cult of the sun god Mithras, initiates were led into the pit of a *taurobolium* where they were drenched in the blood of a sacrificed **bull (979)**. Of all animal sacrifices, the bull was the most important and valuable in the ancient world. In Indo-Iranian mythology, Mithras slaughtered a primordial bull whose blood and semen provided the germinating force for life on earth.

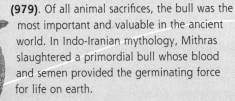

With sacrificial meaning, the **lamb (980)** is one of
the earliest symbols of Christ. Prophets such as Isaiah
had described the coming Messiah as a lamb. It is also a
significant sacrificial and redemptive symbol in the Islamic
rites of Ramadan. Important sacrificial animals in many
other cultures include the ram, horse, ox, buffalo, goat
and dog.

981 SELF-SACRIFICE

Self-sacrifice was widely thought to heighten the symbolism
of the act of sacrifice. Outside of the Christian tradition,
there are countless stories and legends in which divinities
are moved by this ultimate act of selflessness. A famous
example in Indian tradition is the sacrifice of Holika, sister
of a king who ordered his own son to be burned alive for
refusing to worship him. Holika saved the young prince's
life at the expense of her own when she joined him on his
pyre while he himself was miraculously saved from the
flames as a divine reward for her sacrifice.

The symbolic theme of female self-immolation, based on
a myth in which Shiva's first consort, Sati, sacrifices herself
in fire, led to the practice of ritual *sati* or **suttee (982)**, out-
lawed by the British in 1829 in an effort to suppress the
burning of widows.

983 SCAPEGOAT

A particularly unpleasant form of sacrifice in the ancient world was the custom of atonement through the punishment and killing of a scapegoat, used as a symbol of other people's

failures or transgressions. The pioneering anthropologist J.G. Frazer cited the flogging and burning of human victims chosen as scapegoats for rulers whose countries had been overwhelmed by military or natural disasters. Frequently the victim was a simpleton, chosen as an inverse symbol of the king. Traces of this can be found in the much later tradition of kings keeping a **fool (984)** at their side, a clown or jester who skilfully played the role of a scapegoat,

LE·FOU

often shrewdly pointing out administrative follies for which he pretended to take the blame.

Some English kings provided their sons with a **whipping boy (985)** who was chastised as a symbolic way of punishing the princes themselves for misconduct.

The name scapegoat came from the Hebrew custom of sending into the wilderness a "goat for Azazel" – a desert demon – at Yom Kippur (the Day of Atonement). Christian doctrine effectively presents Jesus as a scapegoat for the sins of humanity. His "crown" of thorns had ancient precedents in the mocking

wreaths placed on the heads of
other scapegoats killed to atone
for a king's failings.

986 PILGRIMAGE

Expiation or purification were and still are among the several
symbolic motives for pilgrimage. The objective is to set aside
ordinary life for a period and undertake an often testing
journey to a place in which supernatural forces are thought
to concentrate themselves.

987 FORTY

A period of 40 days had extraordinary symbolism in the
ancient world as a symbol of purification, spiritual testing,
penance and abstention. Some symbologists trace this back
to Babylonian astronomy and its distrust of the 40 days in
spring when the group of stars called the Pleiades disappeared from view. Christian and Islamic traditions regularly
use "forty days" to mean "a long enough period". This was
also widely thought to be the period of time it took for the
dead to disappear entirely.

  These traditions are behind the **quarantine (988)**,
a 40-day ban imposed on ships from plague countries
by the port of Marseilles in the 14th century.

DIVINATION

989 ORACLES

Precognition is one of many magical feats accepted by the ancients as part of their belief that the natural and supernatural worlds formed an indivisible whole. But from the earliest times, symbolism was used to bolster the credentials of prophets, priests or shamans whose superior knowledge, intuitive powers or sheer craftiness made them successful seers. Oracles, such as Delphi in Greece, dedicated to Apollo, symbolized the presence of a divinity answering questions through the voice of a human mouthpiece, or through the casting of lots to receive pre-prepared replies, or through the medium of dreams.

Dreams (990) are as ambiguous as oracular advice usually proved to be. Although regarded since the earliest times as omens of future events, they are open to such a range of symbolic interpretation that modern analysts will cheerfully suggest that a given dream may mean one thing or its complete opposite.

991 I CHING

One of the oldest and most subtle systems of divination is the *I Ching*, or *Book of Changes*, which symbolizes the Chinese belief that wise action in

See also:

991 Duality and Union, p.282

life depends on the balancing of two opposing but comple-
mentary forces. The person consulting the book casts yarrow
sticks or coins to determine patterns of three broken or
continuous lines (trigrams) and hexagrams (six such lines),
eventually making up 64 permutations of yin and yang
forces thought to cover the whole range of fundamental
human situations. The book decodes these patterns in such
a way that the questioner or clairvoyant acting for them is
led to think deeply about the possible outcome of any
action. Effectively, it is a system of self-examination.

992   TAROT

As with oracles and the *I Ching*, the reputation of the Tarot
pack is based on the flexibility with which it can be interpreted. The cards used, dating back to the late
14th century, are packed with ancient symbols capable of many shades of meaning.
For an intuitive fortune-teller, they provide
a much more poetic means of prediction
than the consultation of tea leaves, entrails,
sheep shoulder blades, patterns of bird
flight, numbers, clouds or the numerous
other entertaining methods of attempting
to divine the future.

993 ZODIAC

The majesty of the night sky provided early soothsayers with the grandest of all foundations on which to build a symbol system purporting to forecast the course of life on earth. Greek astronomers of the 2nd century BCE produced the first zodiac – meaning a set of animals and beasts of fable representing important constellations within the relatively narrow belt of the sky along which the sun appears to move during the year. The belt symbolized a force-field, and it is on this symbolism that astrology was based – a belief that certain patterns of alignment between celestial bodies at the moment of a person's birth will affect their character and likely actions.

Although modern astronomy finds this idea preposterous, the rulers of some countries still feel comforted if an astrologer tells them the relative positions of the sun, moon or planets against the reference background of the stars is auspicious for a proposed course of action.

See also:

994 Protection, p.25
995 Fertility, p.49;
Health, p.84

994–1000 WOOD AND WATER

The two natural elements most often associated with divination are **wood (994)** and **water (995)** – literally so in dowsing. The use of a forked stick to find hidden water is known from ancient Egypt and China. Symbolically, the wood usually thought to be most effective for dowsing was **hazel (996)**, a traditionally magical wood in many cultures, although **willow (997)** and **peach (998)** were other shade trees that were popular. Scientific monitoring of successful dowsers suggests that human sensitivity to the friction of water moving underground is more important than the instrument used.

Hazel was also linked to the **magic wand (999)** of countless fairy stories which influences the future by making wishes come true. This tradition stems from animist beliefs

in benevolent tree spirits, and from the fertility symbolism of the rod. Similarly, the **wishing well (1000)**, into which coins are thrown, can be traced back to Celtic rituals in which gifts were cast into water to invoke the help of water deities.

1001 REFLECTIVE SURFACES

Transparent or reflective surfaces had clairvoyant symbolism almost every-where. The still water of lakes was seen as a two-way mirror, symbolically allow-ing allowing humans to communicate with water or underground spirits.

Magicians were thought to be able to see both past and future events in mirrors, a superstition still very much alive in 16th-century France, where Catherine de Médicis' astrologer Ruggieri was said to have shown the queen the fate of three sons in the mirror of a Chaumont tower room. Asian shamans consulted reflective plates aimed at the moon or sun to read the future.

See also:

1001 Bad Luck, p.79

INDEX

Notes: The qualities that form topics in this book (such as fame) appear only after the symbols that represent them. If the reader is interested in the quality itself, please refer to the main contents. For reasons of space, only part of the section headings are given in the index – "fame" instead of "fame and fortune". Capitalization of such a quality (Fortune) indicates the personification of it. Major entries are given in **bold**.

acacia, immortality 328
acorns: fertility 52; wisdom 210
    see also oak trees
Adam and Eve: mortality 35;
    nakedness, innocence of 165;
    snake, temptation 155–6
Adonis, with anemone 257–8
agates: fortitude 186; protection
    21; wealth 67
Agnus Dei, salvation **317–8**
Ahura Mazda: goodness 144;
    winged disk, with 308
Akhenaten, sun assoc. 102
albatrosses, fame **74**
alchemy: metallurgy 360; transformation **341–2**
Allah, as light 304
almonds: chastity **200**; wisdom 210
Amalthea, fecundity 60–1
amaranths, immortality 327–8
amber: fortitude 186; health 84
ambrosia, immortality 329
amethysts, temperance 187
Amun, ram assoc. 93
anchors: as disguised cross 174;
    dolphins, combined with 318;
    Hope, with 177; Prudence, with
    205; salvation **318**

anemones: mortality 36; mourning
    257–8
angels: goodness **144–6**; types 146
Anger **247**
animals: see specific animals
ankh: salvation 317; union **284**
Anubis 10–11; death 299
ants, health 81
apes: holding mirror, pride **194**;
    lust, in Christianity 240
Aphrodite/Venus: apples, with 238;
    beauty 130; doves, with 129,
    235; Helen of Troy, with 131;
    Love 224; pearls, with 55, 132,
    232; pears, with 237; rosemary,
    with 214–5; roses, with 132,
    229; shells, with 125; swans,
    with 236 see also Cupid
Apis, fertility 47
Apollo: laurel, with 85, 279; light,
    with 304; peony, with 85
"apple of Carthage": fertility 51 see
    also pomegranates
apples: Aphrodite/Venus, with 238;
    fertility 51; love 237–8
archangels 146
arches, triumphal, victory **277**
Ares: horses, with 47; red, with 113;
    War 272–3; wolves, with 184
Aries: fertility 48 see also rams; zodiac
arks: protection 25–6; salvation **320**
arms, power 91
Artemis: chastity 196; crescents,
    with 196; moon, with 123
ashes: humility 189–90; mourning
    255–6; rebirth 335
ash trees: ascension 351 see also
    Yggdrasil
asphodels: health 85; melancholia
    258; mourning 257
asses, lust 243
Astarte, doves assoc. 129, 235
Athene: olive, with 62, 206; owl,
    with 136, 206; snakes, with 206;
    wisdom 206; wolves, with 184

Atlas, strength 108
Attis: chastity 200; maypole, with 118
Aurora, hope 179
Avarice **192**
axes: authority **96**; disguised cross
    174 see also fasces
axis mundi **348**
Aztecs: gods and goddesses see
    individual deities; rain, fertility 50

Ba, soul 323
baboons: Thoth 207; wisdom **206**
Bacchus see Dionysus
bamboo 251
banyan tree, fecundity 62
baptism, purification **358**
bare feet, humility **190**
basilisks: evil **157** see also dragons;
    snakes
Bastet, femininity 127
bats: envy, with 246; Envy, with 246;
    evil **160–1**; fame 72; health
    160–1; vampires 161
beans, fecundity **62**
beards, masculinity **118–9**
bears: Artio, with 109; femininity
    126; fortitude 183–4; gluttony
    193; lust 240; strength **109**;
    unconscious mind 260
bees: goodness **150–1**; rebirth **338**;
    sovereignty **106** see also honey
begging bowls, humility **190–1**
bells: death **300–1**; protection 26
Bes, protection 26
birds: see specific birds
black (colour): bad luck 77; evil
    152, **152**; mourning **254–5**
blindfolds: Cupid 224; Justice, with
    180
blood 13; purification 363–4; salvation **320**; union **289** see also
    Christianity
blue (colour): cherubs 146; knowledge **134**; love **231–2**; melancholia **255**
bluebirds, happiness 251

boars: fortitude 183–4; lust in Christianity 240; strength **110**

boats, femininity 122

body parts: protection **26–7** see also specific body parts

bones, rebirth **335**

books: knowledge **137**; owl 136–7

bows: and arrows, Cupid 224; strength **113**

bread, union **289**

breasts: charity **173**; fecundity 58

bridges, transformation **346–7**

bridles, Temperance, with 187

broken weapons, peace 269

brown (colour), humility **189**

bubbles, mortality **38**

Buddha, as light 304

Buddhism: breathing, meditation 293; circumambulation, enlightenment 340; "Eight Auspicious Signs" 53; Eight Precious Things, mirrors 148; "Three Blessed Fruits" 51; "Three Senseless Animals" 248; see also these entries: begging bowls 190–1; bells 26; black 152; blue 134; bubbles 38; cows 150; disks 334; eight 73; eye 211; fire 308–9; flowers 340; gold 306; hands 191; lions 29, 181, 183; lotus 53, 340; peacocks 140; pomegranate 51; saffron 189; sceptres 55; seven 210–11; snakes 30; stupa 350; swastika 89; tea **293**; tigers 248; vajra 55; wheels 334

buffalo: power 93; wealth 68

bulls: purification, sacrifice 363; fertility 47; masculinity 121; power 93; Zeus, with 93, 121

butterflies: soul **322**; transformation **347**

caduceus: associated deities 30–1; health 80; snakes 30–1, 80; union 288 see also double spiral

calves: innocence **164**; wealth 68

camellia: beauty 132; fortitude 186

candles: divinity in Christianity 309; Faith, with 174; mortality **37** see also lamps; light; torches

canopies, sovereignty 104

carbuncles, love 231

carnation, red, love 229–30

carp, fortitude 184

castles, chastity **203**

cats: beauty **132–3**; black, bad luck 77; evil **159**; Hecate, with 159; Japan 127; snakes, as protection from 127

caul, fame **73**

caves: fecundity 57; transformation **343–4**; unconscious mind **261–2**; womb assoc. 56

cedars: longevity **40**; as Tree of Life 351–2

celibates **197**

Celts: see individual deities & these entries: acorns; boars; cats; cedars; dogs; Druids; gold; green; long hair; maypole; mead; mistletoe; nut-bearing trees; reindeer; rings; sows; spirals; Tir na n'Og; torcs

centaurs, lust **240**

centre, divinity **312–3**

Ceridwen, fecundity 60

Cernunnos, fertility 48

chains: authority **101**; union **285–6**

Chak, fertility 50

chakras, power **92**

Chalchiuhtlicue, fertility 44

chalices, faith 174

chariots: ascension **356**; authority **100–101**

Charity **171**; hearts, with 171; sieves, with 362

Charybdis 129

Chastity **196**; doves, with **202**; pigs, destruction of 243; shields, with 196

chastity, monks' girdle knots 213

cherubim: fire, with 217; protection 28

cherubs 146

Christianity: angelic orders 146; blood and bread 289; Eye of God, sun 307; "laying on hands" 91; see also these entries: acacia; Agnus Dei; anchors; apes; ashes; baptism; bare feet; bats; bears; bees; begging bowls; bells; blood; boars; brown; butterflies; chalice; circles; crosier; cross sign; dew; dogs; donkey; doves; dragons; East; eggs; eight; emeralds; eyes; fallen horseman; fasting; fire; fish; flagellation; font; forty; foxes; gardens,; girdles; gluttony; goats; grapes; hands; holly; horses; ivory; ivy; lambs; lamp or candle; left side; leopards; lion and lamb; mirrors; mountains; one; palm fronds; peacocks; pelicans; phoenix; pigs; poppies; rainbows; rams; scales; scarab beetles; Seven Deadly Sins; snakes; springs; swords; toads; Tower of Babel; triangle; unicorns; Virgin Mary; wells; whales; wheat; white; wind; wine; wolves see also; Jesus Christ

chrysanthemums, longevity **42**

cicadas, immortality **329**

circles: goodness **146–7**; union **285**, **287**

circumcision, transformation 344–5

clocks: mortality 37; stopping, mourning 259; Temperance, with 187

clouds: fecundity **58**; happiness **253**

cobras: protection 30; uraeus, power 89 see also snakes

cockatrice, evil **157**

cocks: charity 173; fortitude 184; protection **29**; vigilance **138–9**

coffins, protection 26

coins, death 299

comets, death **301**

compasses, justice **180–1**

coral, health 83–84

corn: fertility **51**; rebirth **339**

cornelian, fortitude 186

corniculum 184

cornucopia: fecundity 61; peace **269**; Peace, with 269

corona, divinity 304

cosmic soul 324

cowrie shells: femininity 125; wealth **66**

cows: fecundity **59**; femininity 126; goodness **150**; happiness 251; Hathor, with 58; Hera/Juno, with 59; Jainism 150; Krishna, with 126; Nut, with 58

cranes: fidelity **214**; longevity **41**; vigilance 139

cremation, ascension **354**

crescents: Artemis/Diana, with 196; Byzantium 21–2; chastity 196; Egypt 22; Hecate 21–2; Islam 22; protection **21–2**

crocodiles, transformation 345

Cronus, melancholia 254

crooks, authority **97**

crosiers (crooks), authority **97**

crosses: Agni, with 174; ankh 317; Chi-Rho 177, 317; of light, divinity 304; Cross of Lorraine 316; crucifix 316; crux dissimulata 174; crux immissa 177; disguised cross 174; faith **174, 177**; Greek cross 316; Hinduism 174; salvation **316–7**; sign of, protection **22**; Tree of Life 317; Y-shaped 317

Crown of Stars 310

crowns, sovereignty **104–5**

crows: bad luck **78**; Odin/Wodan, with 274–5; sun assoc. 78; war and victory 274–5

crucifix, salvation 316

crystal, chastity 203

cubes, truth **170**

cuckoos, wealth **69**

Cupid: blindfold and bow 224; doves, with 235; Love 224; lute, with 228 see also Aphrodite/Venus

cups, overturned, mortality **37–8**

Cybele: chastity 200; femininity 122–3; maypole, with 333

cyclops, anger 248

cypresses: Hades/Pluto, with 259; immortality 328; melancholia **258–9**

Daikoku, wealth 64

dances, death **296–8**; union **288–9**

Daphne, chastity 196

date palms, fecundity 62

dawn, hope **214**

Death **294–5**; mortality 37

death ships **298–9**

Deceit 166

deer: love **237**; purity **218–9**

Demeter, rebirth 339

devils, evil **154** see also Satan

dew, purity 218

diadems, sovereignty 105

diamonds: chastity 203; fidelity 214; goodness 148; health 83; love **231**; protection 21; purity 221; truth 169

Diana see Artemis

Dionysus 26; banyan tree 62; dolphins, with 345; eggs, with 336; grapevine assoc. 63; lust 241; protection 26; rebirth 332; wine, with 345

disks: divinity **308**; rebirth 334

dogs: Cerberus 140; Christianity 212; death 299; Fidelity, with 212; fidelity **212**; Parsees 299; vigilance **140**

dolmens, immortality 325

dolphins: anchors and tridents, combined with 318; Dionysus, with 345; Mediterranean, death

300; salvation **318**; transformation 345

donkeys, humility **191**

double spiral: union **288** see also caduceus

doves: Aphrodite/Venus, with 129, 235; Chastity, with **202**; femininity **129**; Holy Trinity 311; love 235; peace 266; Peace, with 266; phallus, depiction by 235

dragon disk, union **285**

dragons 9; ascension 355; egg guarding 66; evil **156–7**; goodness **148–9**; mercury, with 342; Satan, with 156; slaying of 156–7; vigilance **138** see also basilisks; snakes

dreams, as oracles 368

Druids: acorns, fertility 52; mistletoe, fertility 53; oak trees, fertility 53 see also Celts

drummers, death 296

ducks, fidelity **214**

dwarfs: fecundity 57; unconscious mind 263

eagles: claws, ascension 355; countries and culture 275; soul 323; sovereignty 105, 107; war 275

Earth: fecundity **56–7**; mother 25; protection **25**

East, rebirth **336**

"Easter bunny", fertility 49

ebb tides, death 299

eels, fertility 48

eggs: Christianity 335; Dionysus/Bacchus, with 336; rebirth **335–6**; wealth 64, 66

eight: fame 73; rebirth 337

elder, protection 21

elephants: Africa 137; chastity **201**; China, strength 110–11; goodness **149–50**; happiness 251; knowledge **137**; sovereignty 107; wealth 69

emeralds: Christianity, hope 178;

fertility 54–5; fidelity 214; health 83; protection 21

envy 192

Envy, 245; bats, with 246; heart, eating of 245; Invidia 246; scorpions, with 245; snakes, with 245

Eostre, fertility 59

Eros (Love) 224

eyes: Buddhism 211; Christianity 311; Eye of God, sun 307; vigilance 140; wisdom 211

Faith 174

falcons: Egypt 107; hope 179; Peru 107; sovereignty 107; war and victory 275

fallen horsemen, pride 194

fans, authority 98–9

fasces: authority 97–8 see also axes

fasting: purification 359–60; death 296; religions 359

The Fates, mortality 35

father: masculinity 114; supreme being 310

Father Time: mortality 37; Saturn (god), accretion with 254; truth as daughter 166

Faunus see Pan

feather: justice 181; Ma'at 180–1

feet, bare, humility 190

Fidelity 212

fig trees: fecundity 61–2; Shiva and Vishnu, with 62; as Tree of Life 351–2

fire: cherubim, with 217; Christianity see Christianity ; divinity 308–9, 309; heart, with 226; Love, with 224; purification 359; purity 217–8; rebirth 331; salamander, with 361; transformation 341

fish: fertility 11, 311; fertility 49; wealth 66

five: bad luck 76; harmony 290

flagellation, purification 360

flags, war 273–4

flail, authority 99

flames see fire

flaming torch, freedom 271

fleur-de-lis, sovereignty 103–4

flowers: beauty 132; Buddhism 340; chastity 201; enlightenment/transformation 340; femininity 122; fertility 53–4; love 228–30; mortality 36; peace 267; Victorian code 228–9 see also specific flowers

flutes, love 227–8

fly whisk, authority 98–9

font, faith 174

fools, as scapegoat 366

forests, unconscious mind 260–61

Fortitude 182; pillars, with 183

Fortuna 71

Fortune, fame 71–2

forty: purification 367

Fountain of Youth, love 233–4

four: 11–12; Egypt 12, 91; power 90

foxes: deceit 166; evil 161–2; gluttony 193; Loki, with 162; Reynard 161; Satan, with 161

Freedom 270; Statue of Liberty 271

frogs: fecundity 58; transformation 347; water assoc. 58

fruits: fertility 51; immortality 326–7; love 237–9 see also individual fruits

fruit trees, longevity 40

full moon, beauty 131–2

Gabriel (archangel), with lilies 146, 165

Gaia: fecundity 56; femininity 122

Ganesha: goodness 149–50; happiness 251; knowledge 137; strength 111

gardens: Asia 233; chastity 204; Christianity 291; fecundity 57; harmony 291; India 233; Japan 291; love 233–4; Persia 233; Virgin Mary, with 57, 204

garlic, protection 31

garnets: fidelity 214; love 231

Geb, fecundity 56

geese, vigilance 139

Gemini 283

gemstones: chastity 202–3; fidelity 214; fortitude 186; goodness 148; health 82–4; love 231–2; protection 21; purity 220–1; truth 169; wealth 66–7 see also individual gemstones

giants: anger 248; authority 101

gingko, immortality 328

girdles (belts), fidelity 213

gnomes, unconscious mind 263

Gnosticism, ouroboros 334

goats: fecundity 60–1; femininity 126; masculinity 121

gods/goddesses see individual deities

gold: Buddhism 306; Celts 230; divinity 306; Egypt 306; Huitzilopochtli 306; Inca 102; love 230; Mexico 306; purity 221; Ra 306; sovereignty 102; sun, with 102, 105; wealth 66–7

golden apples, immortality 326

golden wreaths, sovereignty 104–5

Goliath, anger 248

The Good Samaritan, charity 171–2

granite, fortitude 186

grapes, salvation 320

grapevines, fecundity 62

Great Flood 342–3

Great Mother, femininity 122

green (colour): Celts 178; China 42; envy 246; fertility 54–5; goodness 151; hope 178; Islam 151; longevity 42

griffins: Minoan civilization 28; power 94; protection 28

Hachiman, boar assoc. 184

Hadad, spear assoc. 116

Hades, cypresses assoc. 259

hair: lock of, love 230; long, freedom 271; long, strength 113 haloes, divinity **304–6**

hammers, power 92

hands: Christianity 311; Egypt 91; of Fatima, charity **173**; of glory 91–2; joined palms, humility **191**; joining, marriage 286–7; power **91–2**; protection 26–7

happiness, gods of **72**

hares, fertility 48–9

Hathor: cows, with 58; fecundity 59; femininity 126; fig tree assoc. 61–2

hawks, war and victory 274

hawthorn, chastity 201

hazelnuts, wisdom 209

hazel wood, magic wands 371–2

headless horsemen, death 300

heads: Greece/Rome, protection 25; power **90–1**; shaved, humility **190**

hearts: Charity, with 171; Egypt 168; Envy, eating by 245; fire, with 226; love **225–6**; peach symbolism 168; sun, with 12–13; truth 168; vases, depiction by 226; wisdom **211**

Hecate 21–2, 159; cats, with 159; crescent 21–2

hedgehogs, gluttony 193

Heket, fecundity 58

Helen of Troy 131

hens, charity 173

Hera: cows, with 59; fecundity 59; geese, with 139; peacocks, with 140; storks, with 59

Herakles, strength **108**

herbs, immortality 327

Hermes/Mercury: caduceus 30–1; fame 70; knowledge **134**, **134–5**, 135; protection 25, 26, 30–1; Thoth, with 135

Hermes Trimegistus 207

heroes and heroines, fortitude **183**

herons, rebirth 331

hexagrams: protection 20; union **284** see also Star of David

Hinduism: breathing, meditation 293; circumambulation, enlightenment 340; Eye of God, sun 307; "third eye", wisdom 211; see also these entries: bell; canopies; circle; cross; dew; disks 334; fasting; four; island; knots; lotus; mountains; rice; ropes; sceptres; snakes; soma; square; stepped temples; tortoise; vajra 55; wheels see also individual deities

hippopotamus, strength **110**

holly, hope **179**

Holy Grail, salvation **320–1**

homeopathic symbols **80–1**

honey: goodness 151; purity **219** see also bees

Hope **177–8**

horned animals, power **93**

horns, fortitude **184**

horsemen, fallen, pride **194**

horses: Ares/Mars 47; Christianity, victory 277; death 300; lust **240–1**; power **93**

horseshoes: fertility 47; protect **22**

Horus, wedjat eye 140

hour-glass: Death, with 294; mortality 37

Huitzilopochtli: gold 306; human sacrifice, with 362–3

hyacinths, fidelity 214

hybrids, female **128–9**

hydra, evil **157**

Hypnos 267; poppies, with 257, 267

ibis: knowledge 136; Thoth, with 207; wisdom **206**

Iblis see Satan

I Ching **368–9**; duality/union 282

ikebana, mortality 36

Inari, wealth 64

incense: ascension **353**; Asia 353; Egypt 353; purity **220**

initiation ceremonies, transformation **344–5**

Invidia (Envy) 246

Iris, rainbows, with 354

irises, melancholia **258**

iron, protection **34**

Ishtar 309; Crown of Stars 310; pearls 55; snakes 47–8; stars, with 278

Isis, Crown of Stars 310

Islam: breathing, meditation 293; circumambulation, enlightenment 340–1; Eye of God, sun 307; see also these entries: bell; bridges; crescent; cube; Death; East; fasting; forty; green; hands; Ka'aba; knots; ladders; mirrors; moon; omphalos; one; pigs; Satan; stars; three; washing; white

islands: happiness **253**; peace **267**

ivory: Christianity 220; health 83; purity **220**

ivy, fidelity **215**

Izanagi, spear assoc. 116–7

Izrael, Death 295

jackals 10; death 299

jade: authority **101**; fortitude 186; goodness 148; health 82; immortality 329; longevity 42; Maoris 101; purity 220–1; truth 169

jaguars: power **94**; sovereignty 107

Jainism: cows, goodness 150; fasting, purification 359

Jambhala, wealth 64

Janus, protection 25

Jesus Christ: fish 11, 311; as lamb 365; as light 304; swastika 313 see also Christianity

Judaism: see these entries: acacia; ashes; fasting; fire; goats; nine; omphalos; one; pigs; rams; salt; unleavened bread; wings

Judas Iscariot 33

Juno see Hera

Jupiter see Zeus

Jupiter (planet) 309

Justice **180**

Ka 323

Ka'aba 170

Kali, as Dark Mother 123

karashishi: justice 183; protection 29

keys: authority **99**; Fidelity, with 212

Khepri, scarab, with 338

kings, masculinity **119–20**

knights, fidelity **213**

knots: love **234**; marriage 287; monks' girdle 213; obedience, chastity and poverty 213; protection **23**

Krishna: cows, with 126; flames, with 309; flutes, with 227–8; lotus, with 309

kundalini 355–6

labyrinths, unconscious mind **261**

ladders, ascension **349–50**

lambs: children, substitute for 164; Christianity 191; humility **191**; innocence **164**; Jesus Christ, as 365; and lions, peace **268**; sacrifice, purification 364

lamia, envy 245

lamps: Christianity 309; truth **170**

lances: masculinity 116; power 92

lanterns, protection **24**

laurel: Apollo, with 279; health 85; immortality 327; peace 266

laurel wreath: protection 25; Truth, with 166; victory **279**

left side, bad luck **78**

leopards, evil **163**

light: divinity **304**; goodness **144**; knowledge **134**; swans, with 131; truth 170 see also candles

lightning 10; Australian Aborigines 50; divinity **314–5**; fertility 49–50; protection from 32; snake assoc. 48; thunderbird, with 314–5; zigzag assoc. 89 see also thunder

lingams 116 see also phallus

lilies: chastity **200**; fleur-de-lis, with 103; Gabriel (archangel),

with 146, 165; Greece, fertility 54; innocence 165; mourning 257; purity **216–7**; sovereignty 105; Virgin Mary, 165, 200, 216

lions: anger **248**; China, protection 29; courage 6–7; Hercules, with 108; India, justice 181; Japan, fortitude 183; justice **180–1**, 183; and lamb, peace **268**; power **94**; protection **29**; sovereignty 106; sun, with 7, 94; victory 277 see also Buddhism

lizards, soul **324**

lodestone, truth 169

Loki 162

lorelei 129

lotus: beauty 132; Buddhism see Buddhism; Egypt 132; enlightenment 340; fertility 53; Greece 338; Hinduism 340; India 132; Japan 132; Krishna, with 229; love 229; Mexico 338; Middle East 338; rebirth **338**; Rome 338; Tantric Buddhism 229; Taoism 340; vulva, depiction 229

Love **224**; see Aphrodite; Cupid

lozenges: femininity 124; fertility **44**

lunar hare, immortality 326

Lung, Asian dragons 148–59

lust: animals **192–3**; apes 243; asses 243, **243**; bears 240; boars 240; horses **240–1**; pigs 192–3; rams 241–2; centaurs **240**; Dionysus 241; Greece 243; Islam 192–3; minotaurs **242**; Pan/Faunus 241; satyrs **241–2**

Lust **240**

lutes, love 228

lynx, vigilance **139–40**

lyres: harmony 290; love 227

Ma'at 169; ostrich feather and scales, with 180–1

maces, authority **96–7**

magic wands, hazel wood 371–2

magpies: fame **74**; happiness 250

maize, fertility 51

mandalas, harmony **292–3**

mandorla **353**; ascension 353; chastity 200; fertility 44 see also Virgin Mary

mandrake, health 84–5

Marduk 309; fertility 52

marriage **286–7**

Mars: (god) see Ares; (planet) 309

Maya: Chak, fertility 50; five (number), bad luck 76

maypoles: Attis, with 118; Celts 116–7; Cybele, with 333; fertility 46; Hillaria 333; masculinity 117–8; rebirth **333**

mead, immortality **329**

Mercury see Hermes/Mercury

mercury (metal) 342

Mercury (planet) 309

mermaids 129

metals **66–67** see individual metals

meteorites, truth 170

Michael (archangel): archangel 146; dragons, slaying of 156–7; scales and sword, with 169

milk: fecundity **57–8**; purity 216

Minerva see Athena

minotaurs, lust **242**

mirrors: apes, held by **194**; broken, bad luck **79**; chastity **203–4**; China 148; Christianity 147; divination 373; goodness **147–8**; Islam 147; Prudence, with 205; Shintoism 147–8; truth **168**; Virgin Mary, with 203–4

mistletoe: Druids 53; fertility **53**; health 85; protection 25

Mithras: bulls, fertility 47; light, with 304; sacrifice, with 363; sun, with 307

moon: Artemis/Diana, with 123; chastity 196; China 326; divinity **308**; femininity **123–4**; fertility **44**; full, beauty **131–2**; immortality **326**; harvest moon, fertility 44; Islam 326; masculinity

123; Oceania 123; Queens, with 124; rebirth 334–5; Sumeria 123; triangles, representation by 285; unconcious mind 263; Virgin Mary, with 123, 308

Morpheus, poppy assoc. 257

mothers: Dark Mother 123; Earth 25; femininity 122–3; fertility 43–4

mountains, ascension 348–9

mushrooms: immortality 327; longevity 40–1

music, harmony 290

musical instruments: love 227–8 see also individual instruments

myrtle, happiness 251

nails, protection 34

nakedness, innocence 165

narcissus: China 251; happiness 251; Persephone, with 339; rebirth 339

necklaces, union 286

Nekbhet, protection 28–9

Neptune, unconcious mind 263

Night 267

night, peace 267

nightingales, love 234–5

Nike, Victory 275–6

nimbus, divinity 304

nine: China 186; fortitude 186; Judaism 170; Nordic culture 186; truth 170

numbers: fame 72, 72–3 see also individual numbers

Nut: cows, with 58; fecundity 59; fig tree assoc. 61–2

Nyx (Peace) 267

oak trees: Druids, fertility 53; fortitude 186 see also acorns

obelisks: Egypt 116; masculinity 117–8

octagons, rebirth 336

Odin: bear, with 109; boar, with 184; cross, with 274–5; crows,

with 274–5; nine, with 186; oak, with 186; wisdom 208–9

Oedipus, Greek sphinx 208

oils, death 296

olive branch: peace 266; Peace, with 266; Wisdom, with 206

olive leaves, chastity 201

olive trees: Athena/Minerva, with 206; fecundity 62; wisdom 206

omphalos, ascension 355

one (number), supreme being 310–11

onyx, truth 169

opals, fidelity 214

oracles 368

oranges: fame 75; love 238

orbs: power 89; sovereignty 105

orchids: beauty 132; fertility 53–4

Orpheus, love 227

Osiris: fecundity 56; grapevine assoc. 63; rebirth 332

ouroboros, rebirth 333–4

owls: Asia 160; Athena/Minerva, with 136, 206; books, with 136–7; Egypt 160; evil 160; Greece 136; knowledge 136; North American Indians 160; wisdom 206; Wisdom, with 206

ox, strength 111

pagodas, ascension 350

palm fronds: Christianity 278–9; death 295; Rome 278; victory 278–9; Virgin Mary, with 295

Pandora, hope 177–8

Pan/Faunus: evil 154; flutes, with 227–8; lust 241

pansy, love 229

partridges: beauty 132; love 235

Peace: associated symbols 269; Nyx 267; olive branch, with 266

peace pipe 268

peach blossom, virginity 201

peaches: heart 168; immortality 327

peacocks: beauty 132; Buddhism 140; China 103; Christianity 193; Hera/Juno, with 140;

immortality 329; pride 193; Rome 329; sovereignty 103; Tibet 140; vigilance 140

pearls: Aphrodite/Venus, with 55, 132, 232; bad luck 78; beauty 133; chastity 202; fertility 55; health 83; India 83; Ishtar 55; love 232; Rome 83; Virgin Mary, with 202–3; wealth 67

pears, love 237

Pegasus, fame 70

pelicans, charity 172

pentacle, protection 20

pentagram, harmony 290

peony: China, beauty 132; health 85; Japan, fertility 54

Persephone 238; narcissus, with 339

phallus: doves, depiction of 235; fertility 46–7; Greece/Rome, protection 27; masculinity 114, 116; snake, with 99 see also lingams

pheasants, beauty 132

The Philosopher's stone: diamonds, with 221; transformation 341–2

phoenix: charity 172; rebirth 331; victory 277–8 see also Christianity

phyrigian cap, freedom 270

pigs: Chastity, destruction by 243; Christianity see Christianity ; gluttony 192–3; lust 243

pilgrimages, purification 367

pillars: Justice, with 183; strength 111–12

pine trees: immortality 328; longevity 40; cones, fertility 52; Nordic culture, fortitude 186

planets: divinity 309–10 see also individual planets

plants: chastity 201; health 84–5; immortality 327–8 see also specific plants

ploughs, fecundity 56

plums: happiness 251

Pluto, cypresses assoc. 259

Pole (North) star, ascension 351

pomegranates: Buddhism 51; fertility 51; love 238; Rome 51 see also "apple of Carthage"

poppies: Christianity 257; Hypnos, with 257, 267; Morpheus, with 257; mourning **257**

Poseidon, unconscious mind 263

posy, love 228

potbelly, wealth 64

Priapus, protection 26

Pride **192, 193**

Prometheus, flaming torch 271

Proserpina 238

prosperity gods **64**

Prudence **205**; anchors, with 205; mirrors, with 205; sieves, with 362; snakes, with 205; Wisdom, interchangability 205–6

Psyche 322

psychopomps 299

Purgatory, purification 359

purple (colour): Byzantium 103; sovereignty **102–3**

pyramids: Egypt 91; immortality 325; power **90**

Pythagorus, three (number) 211

quails, fortitude 184

Quetzacoatl 354–5

Ra: bee assoc. 106; gold 306; uraeus 89

rabbits, fertility 48–9

rain, fertility 49–50

rainbows: ascension **354**; Christianity 354; Iris, with 354; peace 266; snakes, with 354–5; Tantric Buddhism 354; wealth **67**

Ramadan 359

rams: Amon, with 93; Christianity 242; fertility 48; Judaism 241–2; lust 241–2; masculinity 121; power 92; protection **29**

Raphael, archangel 146

rats, wealth 64

ravens, war and victory 274–5

red (colour): Ares/Mars, with 113; China 75; fame **75**; protection **31**; seraphs 146; strength **113**

reindeer, wealth 68

rhinoceros: Asia, health 82; masculinity 121

rice, fertility 51

riderless horses, death 300

rings: Celts 230; fidelity **213**; love **230**; marriage 286–7; protection **20–1**; Rome 230

rituals, melancholia **259**

rods, authority **99**

Romulus and Remus 283; banyan tree 62; she-wolf, suckling by 126; Virgin Mothers 197

ropes, ascension **355–6**

rosemary: Aphrodite/Venus, with 214–5; fidelity **214–5**

roses: Aphrodite/Venus, with 132, 229; beauty 132; divinity 313; mortality 86; mourning **257**; red, love 229; Rome 257; white, respect 229; yellow, jealousy 228–9

Round Table, union 287

rubies: China 231; fortitude 186; health 82–3; India 42; Japan, love 231; longevity **42**

rudders, authority **100**

runes, protection **32**

sacrifices: animals 362–4; purification **362–4**; humans 362–3; Mithras, with 363

saddles, peace **268**

saffron (colour), humility **189**

St. Anthony, celibacy 197

St. George, dragon-slaying 156–7

St. John the Evangelist, books assoc. 137

salamanders: fire and sulphur, with 361; purification **360**

salmon: strength 109; wisdom **209–10**

salt: protection 32; purity **221**

Samson, 112, 113

sapphires: love **231–2**; truth 169

Satan: Ahriman 144, 153; basilisk, with 157; cats, with 77; dragons, with 156; evil **152–3**, 154; fame **75**; foxes, with 161; Lucifer, with 153; Mephistopheles with 154; pride **194**; Shaitan 153; snakes, with 155–6; thirteen (number) assoc. 76; witches sabbaths, with 155

Saturn: (god), melancholia **254**; (planet) 309

satyrs: evil 154; lust **241–2**

scales: Archangel Michael, with 169; Christianity 169; justice **180–1**; Ma'at, with 169, 180–1; Themis, with 180; truth 169

scapegoats, purification **365–7**

scarab beetles, resurrection **338**

sceptres: Buddhism 55; dorje 55; fertility **55**; Hinduism 55; sovereignty **105**; thunderbolt assoc. 55

scorpions: Envy, with **245**; health 81

Scylla 129

sea: femininity 122; fertility 49–50; unconcious mind **262–3**

Sekmet 127

seraphs 146

serpents see snakes

Seth, leopards assoc. 163

seven: Arab that. 33; Buddhism 210–11; Japan, fame 72; protection **33**; wisdom **210–11**

Seven Deadly Sins 192; avarice 192; envy 192; gluttony, as animals **192–2**; lust see lust ; pride see pride **194**; sloth as animals **192–3**

Shamash: stars, with 310; winged disk, with 308

shears, mortality 35

shells: Aphrodite/Venus, with 125; femininity 124–5; wealth **66**

shields: Chastity, with 196; Wisdom, with 206

Shiva: bull assoc. 93; death 297–8; fig trees, with 62;

flames, with 309; lignam, with 116; suttee, with 364; trident, with 312; trimurti 312
sickles, Death assoc. 294
sieves, purification **362**
silver: chastity 196; hope **178**; Queens, with 124
six: fame 73; unity 284
skeleton, Death 294
skulls, mortality **38**
Sleep (Hypnos) 267
sloth, animals **192–3**
snails, sloth 193
snakes 9; Adam and Eve, temptation of 155–6; ascension **354**; Athena/Minerva, with 206; Buddhism 30; cats, as protection from 127; Christianity 240; deceit 166; Envy, with **245**; evil **155–6**; fertility 47–8; forked tongue, deceit 166; garlic, as protection from 32; health 80–1; Hinduism 30; immortality 327; Ishtar 47–8; lightning assoc. 48; Lust, with 240; Middle East 206; mortality **35**; phallus, with 99; plumed, ascension 354–5; protection **30–1**; Prudence, with 205; rainbows, with 354–5; rebirth 334; rod, with 99; Rome 80–1; Satan, with 155–6; transformation 344; Virgin Mary, destruction by 155; wisdom **206** see also basilisks; caduceus; cobras; dragons; ouroboros
soil, fecundity 56–7
soma, immortality **328–9**
soul: **322**; universal soul 324
sows, fecundity **60**
spears, masculinity 116–7
sphinx: lion/sun assoc. 94; power 7; protection 28; wisdom **208**
spiders, wealth 67
spirals: Celts 288; fertility **54**; Polynesia, tattos 54; power **89**

springs: fertility 49–50; purity 218; salvation **321**; wisdom **208–9**
squares, union **285**
stags: fertility 48; longevity **40**; masculinity 121
stained glass, divinity 304
stars: of David 284; divinity 309; five-pointed, victory **278**; of Lakshmi 20; Shamash, with 310
Statue of Liberty (Freedom) 271
still life, mortality 36
stones: black, evil 152; fortitude **186**; good 148; omphalos 355
storks: fecundity **59**; longevity 41
storms, anger **247**
strawberries, love 239
stupa, ascension 350
sulphur, salamander assoc. 361
sun: Akhenaten, with 307; China 78; crow, with 78; divinity **306–7**; as Eye of God 307; gold, with 102, 105; heart, with 12–13; Hinduism 307; Islam 307; lions, with 7, 94; Mithras, with 307; obelisks, with 116; Peru 307; pheasants, with 132; Rome 307; sovereignty **102**; wheels, with 89
supreme being **310–11**
swans: Aphrodite/Venus, with 236; beauty **131**; light, with 131; love **236**; Zeus/Jupiter, with 236
swastikas 9; Buddhism 89; as disguised cross 313; Jesus Christ 313; Nazi Party 89; power **88**
swords: Archangel Michael, with 169; Christianity 169; Death, with 294; truth **169**

Taiji Tu **282**
Tantric Buddhism: chakras, power 92; lotus 229; rainbows, ascension 354; yantra, harmony 293; yoni, femininity 124

Taoism: eight (number), fame 73; fasting, purification 359; lotus, enlightenment 340; water, wisdom 210; yin-yang symbol 282
Tarot cards **369**; thirteen 76
tattoos: Dayaks 34; Maoris 89; protection **34**; spirals: fertility 54; power 89
Tawaret, strength 110
tea, harmony **293**
Temperance **187**
tetramorphs, protection 26
Thanatos (Death) 294
Themis, scales 180
thirteen, bad luck **76–7**
thistles, longevity **42**
Thor: hammer, with 92; lightning, with 314
Thoth 207; baboon, with 207; Hermes/Mercury, with 135; ibis, with 207; knowledge 135–6
three: fame 72–3; Islam 73; wisdom **211** see also triangles
The Three Graces 131
thrones, sovereignty **104**
thumbs, power 92
thunder: divinity **314–5**; fertility 49–50 see also lightning
thunderbird, lightning, with 314–5
thunderbolts, fertility 55
tigers: anger **248**; Buddhism 248; power **94**; protection **30**
time, mortality **37**
Tir na n'Og 178, 253
Tlaloc, fertility 50
toads: China, health 81; evil **159–60**; Lust, with 240
tomahawk, authority 96
tomato, love 237
tongues: Dyaks, fertility 46–7; Egypt, protection 26
topaz, fidelity 214
torches: freedom 271; masculinity **117** see also candles
torcs, masculinity **118**
tortoise, strength 111

totems, strength **108–9**

towers: of Babel, pride **195**; chastity **203**

Tree of Life: ascension **351**; birds, with **352**; cedar as 351–2; fig tree as 351–2; salvation/ redemption 317

trees: divination **370–1**; fecundity **61–2**; fertility **52**; fortitude **186**; immortality **327–8**; longevity **40**; nut-bearing, wisdom **210**

triangles: China 124; femininity **124**; Holy Trinity 311; moon, representation of 285; power **90**; union **285** *see also* three

tridents: disguised cross 174; dolphins, combined with 318

trimurti **312**

trumpets, fame **71**

Truth **166**

turquoise (stone), fortitude 186

turtles, longevity **41**

twilight, melancholia 255

twins: duality **283**; *see also* Romulus and Remus

unicorns: chastity **198**; health **82**

unleavened bread, purif. 359–60

uraeus, power **89**

vampires 161; protection from 32

vases: femininity 122; as hearts 226

veils, protection 24

Venus see Aphrodite

Venus (planet) 309

Vestal Virgins, celibacy 197

Victory **275–6**

Vigilance **138**

violet (colour): humility 189; temperance **187, 189**

violets (flower): temperance 187; Virgin Mary, with 189

Virgin Mary 197–8, 198; Crown of Stars 310; gardens, with 204; fecundity 57; irises, with 258;

lilies, with 165, 200, 216; mirrors, with 203–4; moon, with 123, 308; palm fronds, with 295; pearls, with 202–3; snakes, destruction of 155; violets, with 189; white hart, with 219 *see also* mandorla

Virgin Mothers **197–8**

virgins (pagan) **196**

Vishnu 30; boar, with 184; disks, with 308; fig trees, fecundity 62; flames, with 309; snake 30; trimurti 312

volcanoes, anger **247**

voyages, death **298**

vultures, protection **28–9**

vulva: femininity **124**; lotus as 229

walnuts, wisdom 210

War **272–3**

washing: innocence **165**; Islam, purification 358

water: divination **370–1**; fecundity 58; fertility **49–50**; frog assoc. 58; health **84**; purification 358; purity 218; Taoism 210; transformation **342–3**; wisdom **208–9**

weapons: broken, peace 269; masculinity **116–7**; power 92

wedding cake, marriage 286–7

wells: femininity 122; salvation 320; wishing, divination 372

werewolves, evil 163

whales, rebirth **336**

wheat 339

wheels: Fortune 71–2; power **88**; rebirth **334**; as sun symbol 89

whipping boys, as scapegoat 366

whirlwinds, ascension **356**

white: cowardice **280–1**; divinity **306**; elephants, wealth 69; feather, cowardice 280–1; flag, surrender 280; white hart 219; innocence **164–5**; mourning **254–5**; purity 216

wind: divinity **315**; mortality 36

wine: Christianity 345–6; Dionysus, with 345; transformation **345–6**

winged disk, Shamash, with 308

wings: fame **70**; protection **28**

Wisdom **205–6**; associated symbols 206; Prudence 205–6

witches, evil **154–5**

Wodan see Odin

wolves: Christianity 162; death 299; evil **162–3**; femininity 126; gluttony 193; Greece/ Rome, fortitude 184; North American Indians 299; Rome, victory 277

wombs: cave assoc. 56; fecundity 56; protection **25–6**

women, femininity **122**

wood: divination **370**, **371–3**; protection 25

wreaths: golden, sovereignty 104–5; protection **25**

wrens, happiness 250–1

Xochiquetzal, fertility 53

Xoltl, death 299–300

yantra, harmony 293

yellow (colour): China, treachery 281; envy **246**; cowardice 281

Yggdrasil 351 *see also* ash trees

yin-yang symbol, duality **282**

yoke, defeat **280**

yoni, femininity 124

Zeus: bull, with 93, 121; lightning, with 314; nails, protection 34; swans, with 236

ziggurats, ascension **350**

zigzags, power **89**

zodiac **370–1**

Zoroaster: Ahriman 153; light, goodness 144

ACKNOWLEDGMENTS

The publisher would like to thank the following people, museums, and photographic libraries for permission to reproduce their material. Every care has been taken to trace the copyright holders. However, if we have omitted anyone we apologize and will, if informed, make corrections in any future edition.

Key: BAL = The Bridgeman Art Library, London; NG = National Gallery, London

Pages 8–9 De'Vecchi: *Signs of the Zodiac*, ceiling detail, c.1574–75 (Villa Farnese, Caprarola/BAL); **32** Leonardo da Vinci: *Last Supper*, 1495–97 (Sta Maria della Grazie, Milan/BAL); **38** Hans Holbein the Younger: *The Ambassadors*, detail, 1533 (NG, London/BAL); **70** Strozzi: *Personification of Fame*, detail, c.1635–36 (NG, London/Corbis); **76** *Death tarot card* (Private Collection/BAL); **115** Leonardo da Vinci: *Vitruvian Man*, c.1492 (Accademia, Venice/BAL); **125** Botticelli: *The Birth of Venus*, c.1485 (Uffizi, Florence/ BAL); **130** Raphael: *The Three Graces*, 1504–05(Musée Condé, Chantilly/BAL); **135** Correggio: *The School of Love*, c.1525 (NG, London/BAL); **145** Fra Angelico: *Last Judgement*, detail, c.1431 (Museo di San Marco, Florence/BAL); **176** Crane: *Pandora's Box*, 1910 (Bibliothèque des Arts Decoratifs, Paris/BAL); **195** Van Valckenborch: *The Tower of Babel* (Towneley Art Gallery & Museum, Burnley/BAL); **199** *Lady and Unicorn* tapestry, c.1500 (Musée National du Moyen Age de Cluny, Paris/BAL); **215** Hughes: *The Long Engagement*, 1859 (Birmingham Museums & Art Gallery/BAL); **225** Master of Lyons: *Maids and Winged Hearts*, c.1500 (British Library, London/BAL); **232–3** Italian School: *The Fountain of Youth*, c.1600 (Phillips Auctioneers/BAL); **239** Bosch: *Garden of Earthly Delights*, c.1500 (Prado, Madrid/BAL); **256** Le Moyne de Morgues: *Corn Poppy*, c.1568 (V & A Museum, London/BAL); **271** Delacroix: *Liberty Leading the People*, detail, 1830 (Louvre, Paris/BAL); **272–3** Botticelli: *Venus and Mars*, after 1485 (NG, London/BAL); **292** *Hevjara Mandala*, detail (Chester Beatty Library, Dublin); **305** Byzantine School: *Emperor Justinian I*, c.547CE (San Vitale, Ravenna/BAL); **312** *Shiva*, 500–27BCE (British Library, London/BAL); **316** Bernardo Daddi: *Crucifix*, c.1338 (Accademia, Florence/BAL); **357** Russian icon: *Prophet Elijah*, c.1600 (Mark Gallery, London/BAL); **365** Holman Hunt: *The Scapegoat*, detail, 1854 (Lady Lever Art Gallery, Port Sunlight/BAL) **370–1** Agnese: *Signs of the Zodiac*, c.1540 (Royal Geographical Society, London/BAL)

Commissioned artwork credits
Chris Daunt: 13, 17, 27, 43, 45, 50, 59, 60, 98, 107, 119, 127, 153, 158, 173, 185, 243, 252, 269, 276, 286, 288, 298, 314–5, 333, 342–3, 349, 363; **Neil Gower:** 157; **Matt McKenna:** 46, 79, 84, 136, 141, 167, 182, 203, 219, 236, 244, 250, 262, 301, 311, 319, 337, 346–7, 361; **Sally Taylor:** 18, 23, 31, 54, 65, 82–3, 86, 95, 112, 120, 128, 142, 149, 175, 188, 209, 217, 220, 222, 241, 249, 261, 264, 279, 291, 294, 297, 302, 321, 330, 352, 372.